JESUS
LIED

HE WAS ONLY HUMAN

Debunking The New Testament

CJ WERLEMAN

dangerous™
little books

First Published in Great Britain 2010
by Dangerous Little Books www.dangerouslittlebooks.com

Dedicated to Christopher Hitchens

"Thou shalt not bear false witness"
The Ninth Commandment - Exodus 20:16

Contents

Introduction

Shortly following the release of my first book, 'God Hates You. Hate Him Back', I received a number of emails from Christians. While not all received were of the "burn in Hell you scum of Satan" kind, many were. Here is just one example:

"CJ, why write the biography of a God you don't believe in? Why tell people to hate something that you believe is non-existent? Isn't this just as meaningful as 'Leprechauns Hate You. Hate Leprechauns Back'? You don't see Christians writing about non-belief!"

My reply to that kind of statement is that first of all, I am utterly enthralled by religion, all religion! I am constantly surprised, shocked and perplexed that anyone can feel indifference to the most important philosophical questions of all time, the questions that religion purport to answer: "What is the meaning of the human existence"; and "how did we get here?"

These are questions that, I believe, are responsible for religious belief and are ultimately the questions that drive the modern fields of science to ever-greater heights and depths.

My overall objective, as an anti-theist, is to demonstrate that your average Sunday churchgoer has a complete misunderstanding of the particular God they believe in. In their minds, their God is a god of mercy, love, and compassion. A characterization that is ultimately due to Bible illiteracy, charismatic preachers and historical ignorance.

My aim, therefore, in writing 'God Hates You. Hate Him Back' was to bring the Bible back to the people, so to speak, to remind them of who God really is. God, as depicted in His own Bible, is a vindictive, capricious, baby killing, genocidal, merciless, ethnic-cleansing, alpha-male, misogynistic sky-bully. I believe, based on reader and critic reviews, I achieved that aim – that indeed the God of

Abraham, if in the unlikely event he were more than imaginary, is a complete and utter asshole, and certainly a deity worthy of our disdain rather than praise.

Furthermore, I am convinced more than ever that Isaac Asimov, Russian born American author, blew bible-based superstition away with a metaphorical 12-gauge, when he wrote:

"Properly read, the bible is the most potent force for atheism ever conceived."

In an idealistic sense, my goal in writing my first book, was to increase public cognition of God's depraved behavior and malevolent attitudes, at least by our 21st century standards. Ultimately, I wanted to play a small part in providing North America with another nudge on its continued trend in moving away from belief in the God of Abraham, just as the rest of the western developed world appears to be doing.

It is my dream that America, within the next half-century, will look increasingly like the nations of Scandinavia. It is in these nations that belief in any kind of God is confined to less than 30% of their respective populations, resulting in countries such as Sweden, Norway, and Denmark enjoying the fruits of living in societies ranked highest by the United Nations, at least in terms of societal health. (Societal health measured by such metrics as: crime rate; adult literacy; affordable housing; gender equality; teen pregnancy; and access to education).

There was a time when religion ruled our lives; we refer to that period of time as the Dark Ages.

It preceded the Period of Enlightenment, which marked the beginning of the end for religion's relevancy in governing its people. In more modern times, we have seen what the theist worldview looks like, a world where the laws of God are enacted. It looks like Taliban ruled Afghanistan, Saudi Arabia, and Banda Aceh, Indonesia.

Monotheistic religions, the ones written by men (yes, men only) who believed the shovel to be emergent technology, dresses itself up as a magic potion for today and tomorrow's problems. It does this by holding a venerated rear view mirror to ancient times and the moral judgments of bronze aged men. The sixty-six books of the Bible, and the confusing contradictory rambles of the Koran, are less of a guide to modern man for spiritual or moral direction than any number of quasi pop-psycho-babble titles found on our bookshelves today. This includes such entrepreneurial self-styled B.S. gurus as Deepak Chopra, Anthony Robbins, or Dinesh D'Souza. These gentlemen are slick in their ability to sprinkle scientific and psychological vernacular to confuse you into believing their revelations to be profound. In other words, people still buy bullshit... and a lot of it!

Sam Harris places ancient sky-god religion in context of its relevancy to the modern world so eloquently in his book End of Faith:

> *"What if all our knowledge about the world were suddenly to disappear? Imagine that six billion of us wake up tomorrow morning in a state of utter ignorance and confusion. Our books and computers are still here, but we can't make heads or tails of their contents. We have even forgotten how to drive our cars and brush our teeth. What knowledge would we want to reclaim first? Well, there's that business about getting food and building shelter that we would to get reacquainted with. We would want to relearn how to use and repair many of our machines. Learning to understand spoken and written language would also be a top priority, given that these skills are necessary for acquiring most others. When in this process of reclaiming our humanity will it be important to know that Jesus was born of a virgin? Or that he was resurrected? And how would we relearn these truths, if they are indeed true? By reading the Bible? Our tour of*

the shelves will deliver similar pearls from antiquity – like the 'fact' that Isis, the goddess of fertility, sports an impressive pair of cow horns. Reading further, we will learn that Thor carries a hammer and that Marduk's sacred animals are horses, dogs and a dragon with a forked tongue…and when we will want to relearn that premarital sex is a sin? Or that adulteresses should be stoned to death?"

Harris further contends that if the above 'all-humanity memory loss' were to occur, then our relearning of all things of relevance would place the Bible and Koran on the shelf next to Ovid's 'Metamorphoses' and the 'Egyptian Book of the Dead' and Dr Seuss' 'Green Eggs and Ham'.

This now brings me to my objective in writing this book, 'Jesus Lied. He Was Only Human'. As mentioned above, my primary focus of my first book was to remind the world that the God of the Bible *is* a villainess old sod. While I gave a summary of all sixty-six chapters of the Old and New Testament, word space and theme prevented me from taking an in depth analysis of the proclaimed "Son of the Creator", Jesus "bring my enemies before me and slaughter them" Christ (Luke 19:27).

I've written this book as analysis of the New Testament, including an examination of the origins for Christianity; how the Christian Bible came into being; who wrote it; the contradictions and irreconcilable discrepancies of the Gospels; and Paul's domineering influence in shaping the Christian.

By the time you're done reading this book you will know of the arbitrary decisions made by theologically motivated old men in hand picking the "writings of Jesus". It was these old men who chose to include or omit such details as; the respective identities of the Gospels; that Jesus caused great suffering to his followers; how the Gospels, being the four biographers of Jesus, cannot corroborate a single event of Jesus birth, baptism, ministry, arrest, trial, crucifixion, or resurrection; and how Paul started a religion that Jesus, as a fundamentalist Jew of his time, would never had approved of. Thread by thread, we will destroy the fabric that is the myth of Jesus Christ, Superstar. This will leave you with three ultimate conclusions, that:

1. Jesus lied
2. Jesus' biographers lied
3. Christianity is actually founded on talented horse-crappery

It's important to recognize that nothing contained in this book is a revelation. Everything I cover in this book originates either directly from the Bible, or are facts as acknowledged by consensus among scholarly theologians today. What they are not, however, are facts known to Mr. and Mrs. Evangelical Happy-Clapper or your average card carrying Christian in the pews. However, it is my belief that Christianity will continue its downward trend in the United States. Especially as this information, once only known to the intellectual few and the theological protectors of the Church (i.e. the ones smart enough to read the bible they were told to believe in), becomes common knowledge for all.

Christianity remains the largest faith group in the world today, that is if you count Catholics, Protestants, Eastern Orthodox, evangelicals, Mormons, Jehovah's Witnesses, and all denominations remotely connected with Christianity. Yet these groups don't always agree. In fact, some of them strongly disagree with each other that violent confrontation often results -- begging the question: What is Christianity?

Let's go through a quick definition.

The word "Christianity" of course derives from the word "Christ," which literally means "Anointed One." Christians universally believe that the AD 1st century figure named Jesus of Nazareth was the "Anointed One."

(Do not confuse this as the Messiah that starry-eyed twenty-something's proclaimed as Barak Obama) While this definition seems simple enough to us on the outside looking in, it is far from not, judging by the 38,000+ denominations of this religion which persist to this day. The reason for this massive number of dissonance in the teaching of the doctrines is easy to pinpoint; Christianity is complex because the early Christians couldn't agree on any of the central tenets of the story... and still don't 2000 years later. Not helping this is the infinite contradictions and the crude carpentry of tacking together the respective books of the New Testament.

"Christianity makes no sense: 38,000 denominations can't be wrong," would make an excellent bumper sticker! But rest assured Christians have a rebuttal for this philosophical phenomenon. The following is a typical explanation, this taken from a brochure distributed by North Point Ministries, USA:

> *"So, why are there so many different denominations and types of churches? There are several reasons. For starters, let's not forget that denominations are made up of churches and churches are made of people; and sometimes people just don't get along. After all, just because people are Christians doesn't mean they always agree. Moreover, Christians still struggle with pride, selfishness, and stubbornness, and this means they sometimes respond to relational conflict poorly.*
>
> *This has often led to debates and divisions within churches and denominations, which in turn leads to the creation of new churches and denominations. It's an unfortunate situation, but a reality given human nature. Maybe this is why Jesus focused so much on unconditional love and forgiveness as an expression of the kind of people he wants us to be."*

This is the tired and overused, "Jesus was perfect, man is fallible", excuse. But the apology completely misses the target, as the fallibility is contained within the text, the New Testament. Christianity manufactures these divisions because of the irreconcilable discrepancies, illogical assertions, false promises, historical and geographical errors, contradictions, and corrupted texts that constitute the canonized books of this religion. Put simply, Christianity is an argument from errors and ignorance.

We will examine all of these in due course, and as such - the New Testament's inerrancy will dissolve before your very eyes... a magic trick I've been practicing for some time. Thus for now, I will leave you with my favorite religious joke, one which sums up the contradictory and flawed basis for this faith quite expertly:

> *I was walking across a bridge one day, and I saw a man standing on the edge, about to jump off. So I ran over and said, "Stop! Don't do it!"*
> *"Why shouldn't I?" he said.*
> *I said, "Well, there's so much to live for!"*
> *He said, "Like what?"*
> *I said, "Well, are you religious or atheist?"*
> *He said, "Religious."*
> *I said, "Me too! Are your Christian or Buddhist?"*
> *He said, "Christian."*
> *I said, "Me too! Are you Catholic or Protestant?"*
> *He said, "Protestant."*
> *I said, Me too! Are your Episcopalian or Baptist?*
> *He said, "Baptist!"*
> *I said, "Wow! Me too! Are your Baptist Church of God or Baptist Church of the Lord? He said, Baptist Church of God!"*
> *I said, "Me too! Are your Original Baptist Church of God or are you Reformed Baptist Church of God?"*
> *He said, "Reformed Baptist Church of God!"*

I said, *"Me too! Are you Reformed Baptist Church of God, Reformation of 1879, or Reformed Baptist Church of God, Reformation of 1915?"*

He said, *"Reformed Baptist Church of God, Reformation of 1915!"*

I said, *"Die, heretic scum!" and pushed him off.*

A final word, in regards to the title, some may believe it is unnecessary harsh at first glance, but I hope to clarify my reasoning for the choice in chapter one, and hopefully you too will believe the title deserving. If you're a Christian, however, and still believe it's too blasphemous, well, according to your faith, you have no choice but to forgive me anyway.

CJ Werleman
www.cjwerleman.com

CHAPTER ONE

Jesus Lied!

It was CS Lewis who wrote, in *Mere Christianity*, that Jesus had to have been either a liar, a lunatic or Lord. Thus becoming one of the most famous quotes used by both sides of the theological debate. The passage referred to is:

> *"I am trying here to prevent anyone saying the really foolish thing that people often say about Him: "I'm ready to accept Jesus as a great moral teacher, but I don't accept His claim to be God." That is the one thing we must not say. A man who said the sort of things Jesus said would not be a great moral teacher. He would either be a lunatic--on a level with the man who says he is a poached egg--or else he would be the Devil of Hell. You must make your choice. Either this man was, and is, the Son of God: or else a madman or something worse. You can shut Him up for a fool, you can spit at Him and kill Him as a demon; or you can fall at His feet and call Him Lord and God. But let us not come with any patronizing nonsense about His being a great human teacher. He has not left that open to us. He did not intend to."*

Ultimately, CS Lewis made the leap from reason into faith and accepted the presupposition that Jesus had to have been God himself. His next chapter begins with:

> *"We are faced, then, with a frightening alternative. This man we are talking about either was (and is) just what He said, or else a lunatic, or something worse. Now it seems to me obvious that He was neither a lunatic nor a fiend: and consequently, however strange or terrifying or unlikely it may seem, I have to accept the view that He was and is God. God has landed on this enemy-occupied world in human form."*

How he made that personal decision is not for me to speculate. I can only assume he did not read the same Bible that I have before me, for Jesus proved unequivocally to be a lying merchant of false hope and irrefutably a false prophet. Now, the only defense we can lay before Jesus, for his numerous false promises, is that indeed he was a self-deluded madman, to borrow Lewis' term once again. Is that too harsh? Am I over-reaching? Well, let's see. The dictionary defines megalomania as:

> A psychopathological condition characterized by delusional fantasies of wealth, power, or omnipotence. An obsession with grandiose or extravagant things or actions.

Hmm smells like Jesus, doesn't it? My favorite philosopher of all time is Bertrand Russell, and as a matter of fact I have a poster of him positioned near my desk, which doesn't make me gay, not that there's anything wrong with that, famously quipped:

> "The megalomaniac differs from the narcissist by the fact that he wishes to be powerful rather than charming, and seeks to be feared rather than loved. To this type belong many lunatics and most of the great men of history."

Feared rather than loved, huh? Wasn't it Jesus who said, "I have come not to bring peace, but a sword"? Or, how about the following little promise, one that demonstrates eternal suffering, in that oh so special Jesus homo-erotic way:

> "As the weeds are pulled up and burned in the fire, so it will be at the end of the age. The Son of Man will send out his kingdom everything that causes sin and all who do evil. They will throw them into the fiery furnace, where there will be weeping and gnashing of teeth."
> (Matthew 13:38-42 NIV)

The intense and somewhat comical examination of the New Testament will leave you with the understanding, and of this I have no doubt, that Jesus was indeed a liar and a lunatic. And certainly far from the Lord - C.S Lewis would have you believe. Well, possibly the moniker of Lord of the Lies, the Dean of Deceit, the Duke of Delusion would be more apt.

So, what of the lies, then? Certainly, there are varying degrees of lies or mistruths. For example, if Jesus had have promised his disciples, "Alright lads, listen up for a moment. At 7pm tonight I will be at the Temple to trial run my 'Rabbi and a Jebusite walk into a bar' joke. I will meet you guys there" Now, if Jesus got distracted with his messianic chores, or if he fell asleep on the massage table at the Bethlehem Fun Palace, thus missing his 7pm rendezvous with his small band of followers, then we can pass that off as either a little white lie, or more appropriately a scheduling mishap. Moreover, Jesus' mishap, in this example, would have caused his band of dress wearing men little inconvenience.

Possibly, Simon missed his poker game, and Andy, his happy hour shots at the Tyre Tool Shed, but ultimately very little physical or emotional suffering would have been incurred. Hence, Jesus may be forgiven in the aforementioned hypothetical circumstance.

Problem is though; we can find numerous examples in the Bible that give us reason to vilify Jesus on the charge of deceit causing harm. In fact, we can point to an irrefutable case in which Jesus not only misrepresented himself, because he really believed himself to be God, but one that undoubtedly would have caused great suffering to his original band of brothers. But let's first set the scene. Jesus gives the following as part of his long-winded diatribe atop the Mount of Olives:

> "Therefore I tell you, do not worry about your life, what you will eat or drink; or about your body, what you will wear. Is not life more important than food, and the body more important than clothes? Look at the birds of the air; they do not sow or reap or store away in barns, and yet your heavenly Father feeds them. Are you not much more

valuable than they? Who of you by worrying can add a single hour to his life?" (Matthew 6:25-27 NIV)

"Give no thought for the morrow" is the central philosophy of Jesus' teachings. It's olde English for "Don't worry about tomorrow, because I've got that shit covered". Effectively, Jesus is telling us that we need not concern ourselves with thrift, investment, child care, sowing crops, diet, and health. Now, why would he preach such a seemingly, on the surface, absurd life message? Well, the answer to that question comes just a few chapters later in the Book of Matthew, whereby Jesus describes to his disciples what the pending end of times will look like:

"Immediately after the distress of those days, 'the sun will be darkened, and the moon will not give its light; the stars will fall from the sky, and the heavenly bodies will be shaken." (Matthew 24:29 NIV)

Terrifying stuff, huh? But not to worry, our hero will arrive, and because of his unconditional love for us, (unconditional, that is, unless you have been naughty little Jew) he will escort the righteous to heaven:

"At that time the sign of the Son of Man will appear in the sky, and all the nations of the earth will mourn. They will see the Son of Man coming on the clouds of the sky, with power and great glory." (Matthew 24:30 NIV)

The earth's final days will climax with the appearance of a rabbi Jew riding a fluffy white cloud over the skies of Manhattan? Ok, the Bible doesn't give the locale for the prophecy of his return (tough shit for the Mormons who believe he will return to Missouri) but Jesus certainly gives us a date for the promised apocalypse:

"I tell you the truth, this generation will certainly not pass away until all these things have happened. " (Matthew 24:34 NIV)

"Verily I say unto you, That there be some of them that stand here, which shall not taste of death, till they have seen the kingdom of God come with power." (Mark 9:1)

"Verily I say unto you, This generation shall not pass away, till all be fulfilled." (Luke 21:32)

"Verily I say unto you, This generation shall not pass, till all these things be fulfilled." (Matthew 24:34)

There is your smoking gun, people! The slam-dunking of your false prophet! The gunman on the grassy knoll just shot Jesus down. Booya!

As you can see, Jesus promised his followers in no uncertain terms that not only will he return, but he will also take God's children to the kingdom of Heaven before his contemporaries would experience death. With the date of Jesus' death more or less 35 AD, and a generation being no more than an additional forty years, this meant he repeatedly promised his second coming and salvation to all believers prior to the year 75 AD. Well, the year is now 2010, and with no sign of Jesus riding said cloud in the night's sky, he is 1965 years late on his bullshit promise and his early followers, the ones who abandoned their life's desires, their physical and financial health, lay where they fell, buried in the dirt. His true believers would've died with nothing and gone nowhere...

Bertrand Russell put it ever so eloquently in a speech given in 1929, when he said:

"When Jesus said, "Take no thought for the morrow," and things of that sort, it was very largely because He thought the second coming was going to be very soon, and that all ordinary mundane affairs did not count. I have, as a matter of fact, known some Christians who did believe the second coming was imminent. I knew a parson who frightened his congregation terribly by telling them that the second coming was very imminent indeed, but they were much consoled when they found that he was

planting trees in his garden. The early Christians really did believe it, and they did abstain from such things as planting trees in their gardens, because they did accept from Christ the belief that the second coming was imminent. In this respect clearly He was not so wise as some other people have been, and he certainly was not superlatively wise."

We, today, have the luxury of passing this off with numerous nuanced theories but what we can't nuance away is the fact that his teaching, 'Don't worry for tomorrow', would have brought great misery on not only his followers but the founding or early members of the Christian church, as established throughout the Mediterranean by Saint Paul.

Keeping in mind that Paul makes mention of Jesus' promise no less than thirty times throughout his letters to the early Christian churches, as a means of rallying the faithful. In fact, the second coming is a central component of Paul's recruitment pitch, "Look, here ye at this new religion we've started. There was this Jewish dude named Jesus. Well, anyway, he walked on water, fed 5,000 people with two sardines, and his spirit flew into heaven three days after he was executed."

Naturally, a common question from his mostly non-Jewish audience would have been, "If we join, what's in it for us?" To which Paul offered, "Umm, He will return from Heaven to Earth, and we believers will all be given eternal life. Are you with me?" It's a hell of a promise.

With passing time, the founding fathers of the Christian church started to become anxious, as evident by Paul's letters, that the shot clock on forty years (generation) was running down. This anxiety caused many of the early followers of Paul to panic that with their aging, and the term of a full generation approaching, death would precede them witnessing the second coming. Paul responds to their concerns in his Epistle 1 Thessalonians:

"According to the Lord's own word, we tell you that we who are still alive, who are left till the coming of the Lord, will certainly not precede those who have fallen asleep. For the Lord himself will come down from heaven, with a loud command, with the voice of the archangel and with the trumpet call of God, and the dead in Christ will rise first. After that, we who are still alive and are left will be caught up together with them in the clouds to meet the Lord in the air. And so we will be with the Lord forever. (1 Thessalonians 4:15 NIV)

If we return again to the Sermon on the Mount of Olives, a continuance of his speech, the part where Jesus promises a heavenly return before the then current generation would need to make a bucket list, Jesus warns:

"Watch out for false prophets. They come to you in sheep's clothing, but inwardly they are ferocious wolves. By their fruit you will recognize them. Do people pick grapes from thorn bushes, or figs from thistles? Likewise every good tree bears good fruit, but a bad tree bears bad fruit. A good tree cannot bear bad fruit, and a bad tree cannot bear good fruit. Every tree that does not bear good fruit is cut down and thrown into the fire. Thus, by their fruit you will recognize them." (Matthew 7:15-22 NIV)

False prophets, huh? Ok, Jesus we will keep an eye out for them when they come. Wait! I think we found our false prophet, ladies and gentleman. Possibly, a further reason as to why the Jews were less than impressed with Jesus, and let's face it, they were well adept in the prophet business, having identified sixteen of them in the Old Testament from Isaiah to Malachi. Thus, we can presume they knew a prophet when they saw one. Possibly, even better than they can spot a real estate opportunity in lower Manhattan. Thus we can presume that Jesus was as impressive to the Jews as a white man showering in a Jamaican gym.

Further illuminating, is the fact that John makes no reference to the promise of Jesus' second coming in his gospel account. Ask yourself, why? Well, the glaringly obvious reason is the Gospel of John was written, approximately, in 100 AD, which is almost two generations after Jesus had died! As such, this promise would have made little sense, as the original generation was, by that time, in a state of heavy decomposition.

This is why the Apostle John went to such extraordinary lengths to promote the idea of Jesus' supposed divinity. In doing so, he purposely distanced himself from the Synoptic Gospels, by claiming that Jesus was, in fact, God in the flesh. Obviously, when your unique selling point has been scuttled as a consequence of being an obvious fallacy, a new doctrine of divine hope has to be packaged with a pretty new divine ribbon, which is effectively what John did.

Moreover, Jesus' promise to return, "before the current generation would pass" is not the only time Jesus sells his followers up the proverbial river in the New Testament. Unfortunately, for the two billion plus Christians of the world, there are multiple examples, including:

Lie #2

> *"When you are persecuted in one place, flee to another. I tell you the truth, you will not finish going through the cities of Israel before the Son of Man comes."*
> *(Matthew 10:23 NIV)*

The above passage is Jesus speaking to his apostles; he tells them that he will return before they are able to spread the word throughout all of the cities in Israel. Well, the word has now spread throughout all of Israel, and Jesus is yet to return. (Try to find a Jew in Jerusalem that hasn't at least heard of Jesus. I dare you)

JESUS LIED – HE WAS ONLY HUMAN

Lie #3

Matthew writes that the Pharisees and teachers of the Law approach Jesus, asking for a sign to prove that he is who he says he is. Jesus responds sharply:

> *"A wicked and adulterous generation asks for a miraculous sign! But none will be given it except the sign of the prophet Jonah. For as Jonah was three days and three nights in the belly of a huge fish, so the Son of Man will be three days and three nights in the heart of the earth." (Matthew 12:39-40 NIV)*

Jesus, effectively, is telling the Pharisees that the only sign he will give is his resurrection three days after he his dead. Did they, the Pharisees, see this as a sign and a reason to convert? No, and why would they; Jesus was adept only as a reciprocating big talker. Only Jesus' disciples, allegedly, saw it. But it was not Jesus' disciples asking for a sign, it was the Pharisees, the Pharisees living in the then present generation, therefore we can strike this down as another false promise.

Lie #4

Now, as the baseball-loving guy that I am, I'm tempted to just say, "Jesus, three strikes buddy, you're outta here!" But then again, that wouldn't make for a very entertaining book, now, would it? And we've still got so much more of Jesus' personality, which lays unread by the mostly scripturally and historically ignorant masses of Christianity.

We'll delve later into the ill-tempered nature of Jesus, but one such example that invokes the ire of 'meek n mild' Jesus is the scene between him and the Pharisees and Jewish elders. Jesus lets fly with further promises and prophecies during this barbed exchange:

> *"The men of Nineveh will stand up at the judgment with this generation and condemn it; for they repented at the*

preaching of Jonah, and now one greater than Jonah is here." (Matthew 12:41 NIV)

Ooh, did that give you goose bumps, too?

Now, during the time of Jesus, the town of Nineveh had ceased to exist for nearly 600 years. The former city was nothing but a sand pit. This prophecy states that the dead shall rise in judgment with this generation. Exactly which generation was he referring to? Specifically, those Jesus referred to as a, 'wicked and adulterous generation'. And who was seeking the sign? The Pharisees. That was the generation he was referring to, that was the generation he was speaking to. Generation has a very special and specific meaning in the original Greek, and cannot possibly refer to a future generation in any tense that could be translated as 'this generation'.

Lie #5

Later in Matthew, Jesus is before the Sanhedrin. The Jewish elders had assembled to find evidence that they could pin on Jesus so as to expedite a death sentence for blasphemy against him. The High Priest said to Jesus, "I charge you under oath by the living God: Tell us if you are the Christ, the Son of God." Jesus replies:

"Yes, it is as you say," Jesus replied. "But I say to all of you: In the future you will see the Son of Man sitting at the right hand of the Mighty One and coming on the clouds of heaven." (Matthew 26:64 NIV)

Ooh, goose bumps again!

In this instance, Jesus is talking directly to the High Priest. He has promised him that he shall see this happen. Well, the high priest has been dead almost 2,000 years, and therefore we have our fifth deception.

Lie #6

Jesus promised his disciples, repeatedly, that prayer works:

> *"And Jesus answered and said to them, "Truly I say to you, if you have faith and do not doubt, you will not only do what was done to the fig tree, but even if you say to this mountain, `Be taken up and cast into the sea,' it will happen. "And all things you ask in prayer, believing, you will receive." (Matthew 21:21-22 NAS)*

> *"Ask and it will be given to you; seek and you will find; knock and the door will be opened to you. For everyone who asks, receives; and the one who seeks, finds; and to the one who knocks, the door will be opened. " (Matthew 7:7-8 NAB)*

> *And whatever you ask in my name, I will do, so that the Father may be glorified in the Son. If you ask anything of me in my name, I will do it. (John 14:13-14 NAB)*

However, we know with scientific certainty that nothing quite has the failure rate of prayer, unless, of course, God hates amputees. Every day, tens of thousands of Christians claim that they've been the beneficiaries of Jesus' miraculous intervention. Whether the believer received the job promotion, finished first in his math's exam, or finally snared the girl of his dreams. They prayed for their goal and they received. Thus strengthening their belief in the Lord Almighty. But what of the 'other' guy, a Christian too, that missed out on the girl? Did God like him less? Does God show favor? This is what we in the 'I'm smarter than a prayerful Christian' game; call "confirmation bias." But according to the Bible, God doesn't play favorites:

> *"I now realize how true it is that God does not show favoritism but accepts men from every nation who fear him and do what is right." (Acts 10:34-35 NIV)*

Of course, this is contradiction to the book of Genesis whereby God favored Abel over Cain, but that's a whole another story. Let's return to the failure of prayer.

Holding a microscope to the effectiveness of prayer we can make the following conclusion, if prayer works then God hates people who have lost a limb, or who were born without a full set of arms or legs. This hypothesis is so robust that one atheist website posted a US$100,000 reward for any proof that demonstrates God has restored the limb of an amputee via prayer. Quite tellingly, in the more than two years this challenge has stood, not one religious believer has stepped forward to claim the reward money. Who me, surprised? Also, considering that there are more than 50,000 new amputees courtesy of the violent and bloody conflicts in Iraq and Afghanistan, an overwhelming majority of which claim to be Christians, there should be no shortage of takers for an easy few extra bucks. Alas, the prize remains unclaimed.

The amputee question allows us to critically analyze the effectiveness of prayer, and the results are not in the favor of the 'big guy'. The result of applying this blowtorch is that it eliminates the two clouds of uncertainty related to prayer; ambiguity and coincidence.

A clever hypothetical scenario put forward by one particular website, WhyWontGodHealAmputees.com, illustrates this brilliantly:

Let's imagine that your doctor has diagnosed you with an aggressive form of bowel cancer. You opt to take the chemotherapy that your doctor has recommended. As this god-awful remedy of radiation exposure begins you are naturally terrified at the prospect that the number of your days on earth are dramatically falling.

Assuming you are a Christian, you begin to pray to God or Jesus to circumvent all natural laws and enact some divine intervention. So, you pray your ass off, morning and night, before, during and after surgery that your heavenly father will spare you an early visit to the grave... even though, as a Christian, you're taught to believe that you'll go to heaven in the end anyway (I never quite understood why Christians were so afraid of death). I digress.

A few months after the chemotherapy treatment has concluded, your doctor is delighted to tell you that the cancer has gone into remission and that all signs of the life threatening disease have now vanished. Naturally, you give thanks to God for heeding your prayers and your ~~confirmation bias~~ conviction and faith in Jesus is stronger than ever before. Praise the Lord!

But how do we objectively rationalize the above scenario? What saved you from seemingly imminent doom? Well, there are several possibilities. Was it the surgery? The radiation therapy, maybe? How about your body's natural defenses? Or, was it that God circumvented all natural laws in order to directly treat your bowel cancer (but won't lift a finger for the millions living with famine and disease in Africa)?

On the surface the answer to this question seems ambiguous. God may have miraculously cured your disease, as many Christians would believe. But if we presume God is fiction then it had have been one or a combination of the chemotherapy, surgery and/or your natural immune system that cured you.

There is only one way to remove coincidence of prayer from this scenario and that is to eliminate ambiguity. In an unambiguous situation, there is no potential for coincidence and because there is no ambiguity we can actually 'know' whether God is answering the prayer or not. The examination of amputees allows us to completely remove all ambiguity, and in doing so, creating an unambiguous situation where we can see with our own eyes that prayer never ever works.

Therefore, we can be sure that whenever a believer has proclaimed instances of miraculous healing through prayer we can be certain that the possibility of coincidence was present. What we find is that whenever we create an unambiguous situation like this and look at the results of prayer, prayer never works. God never answers prayers if there is no possibility of coincidence.

In returning to CS Lewis' remarks once more, we can conclude that if Jesus lied, as evidently he did, then he cannot be Lord, by process of elimination. Therefore by his standard, Jesus was a liar and a lunatic. 'Liar, liar, pants on fire!'

There is your title…

'Jesus Lied. He Was Only Human'

Now let us move forth and pull apart the fabric of Christianity, thread by thread, using the Gospels and Saint Paul as our collaborators. This will be easier than you think, and oh so much fun.

CHAPTER TWO

How Christianity Started

What I'm about to write in capital letters may come as a big surprise to you, especially if your theological or Bible study is limited to singing a few sweet psalms on Sundays. So brace yourself for a little mind-shift:

*JESUS HAD NO INTENTIONS OF STARTING
A NEW OR NON-HEBREW RELIGION*

Did I just blow your mind? It did for me when I first discovered this fact, a fact that is openly (seemingly proudly) displayed in the scriptures. And I didn't have to search some obscure ancient conspiracy documents to uncover this, it's in black and white, written right there in the Holy book.

Here's the deal: Jesus was a Jew. He was raised by Jewish parents; he observed all the Jewish holidays; he prayed at the Jewish Temple; he prayed to the Jewish God; his followers had to be Jewish. Jesus loved everything Jewy about being a Jew. He loved his Jewishness more than Woody Allen loves his. So much so, that he put his unwavering endorsement behind the Hebrew Bible, the Old Testament:

> *"Do not think that I have come to abolish the Law or the Prophets; I have not come to abolish them but to fulfill them. I tell you the truth, until heaven and earth disappear, not the smallest letter, not the least stroke of a pen, will by any means disappear from the Law until everything is accomplished. Anyone who breaks one of the least of these commandments and teaches others to do the same will be called least in the kingdom of heaven, but whoever practices and teaches these commands will be*

called great in the kingdom of heaven. For I tell you that unless your righteousness surpasses that of the Pharisees and the teachers of the law, you will certainly not enter the kingdom of heaven." (Matthew 5:17-20 NIV)

This is a complete, unflinching, unfaltering sponsorship of all 613 commandments of the Old Testament Law of the 12 tribes of Israel. This quite clearly, and very concisely means that Jesus embraced with both of his respective man bosoms, laws that we today find unashamedly, utterly, completely, totally, morally repugnant. Laws such as:

- Murder your own daughter if she follows Buddha's teachings during her college experimental years. *(Exodus 20:4)*
- Stone to death your son if he tells you to get lost. *(Exodus 20:12)*
- Divorce your newlywed wife if she doesn't sexually please you on your wedding night. *(Deuteronomy 24:1)*
- Murder your newlywed wife on her father's doorstep, if you discover, post nuptials, she is not a virgin. *(Deuteronomy 22:20)*
- If you're a woman and raped, you must marry your rapist, and never divorce. *(Deuteronomy 22:28)*
- Murder your child if you discover they are born gay. *(Leviticus 20:13)*
- Murder your daughter if she does a Saturday shift at McDonalds for a little spare pocket money. *(Exodus 20:10)*

They're but a teeny snippet of some of the more barbaric Hebrew laws that Moses and Jesus embraced. Why? BECAUSE HE WAS A JEW, AND BLOODY PROUD OF IT! Which meant he loved his circumcised penis, and abhorred and disrespected the uncircumcised masses of all other nations.

"Move back you unclean snorkel dicks," is most likely what he yelled when venturing through non-Jewish towns. While you may well think that what I've written here is utterly absurd, the Bible contains more than 200 references to battles waged earnestly between the two alternate models of penis! Seriously!

To be uncut meant you were a filthy foreigner in the eyes of all Jews, of that time. King David even makes mention of Goliath's penis in his pre-battle self-arousal speech. David, prior to becoming King, steps forward to slay the 9 foot tall Goliath with naught but a sling and stone, when none of his much older and bigger compatriots will do so. David screams at his colleagues, embarrassed by their cowardice, "How can you blokes be afraid of this pathetic sod? Look at him. Yeah he's 3 meters tall but look at his dick, he's sporting one of those convertible models. He's like a little girl. I will beat his ass." *(1 Samuel 17:26)* …And he did.

There is no reason for us to mince words. The ancient Hebrews were a tribe of violent, xenophobic bigots! Don't believe me? Read Exodus through Kings. An orgy of ethnic cleansing is illustrated right there for the bloody lusty reader.

A genocidal contempt for all non-Hebrew societies is unashamedly illustrated via the leadership of Moses to Joshua, from David to Solomon. And after all Jesus, so the Bible alleges, was the direct descendent of David. Ethnic cleansing was in his blood. He was Hebrew through and through, right down to the leather straps on his sandals. Let us remind ourselves how the ancient Jews felt about neighboring societies that practiced religion freedom:

> *"If your very own brother, or your son or daughter, or the wife you love, or your closest friend secretly entices you, saying, 'Let's go out and worship other gods', do not yield to him or listen to him. Show him no pity. Do not spare him or shield him. You must certainly put him to death. Your hand must be the first in putting him to death and*

then the hands of the people. Stone him to death because he tried to turn you away from the Lord your God…...Then all Israel will hear and be afraid, and no-one among you will do such an evil thing again."
(Deuteronomy 13:6-11 NIV)

"If you hear it said about one of the towns the Lord your God is giving you to live in that wicked men have arisen among you and have led the people astray, saying, 'Let us go and worship other gods', then you must enquire, probe and investigate it thoroughly. And if it is true and it has been proved that this detestable thing has been done among you, you must certainly put the sword to all who live in that town. Destroy it completely, both its people and its livestock. Gather all the plunder of the town into the middle of the town square and completely burn the town and all its plunder as a whole burnt offering to the Lord your God." (Deuteronomy 13:12-16 NIV)

Moreover, we have New Testament examples of Jesus' wrath and contempt for non-Jews, as depicted in Matthew's narrative of the Canaanite woman brought before Jesus. The woman's daughter is suffering from a high fever. She and Jesus believe she is demonically possessed, which in modern terms most likely means that she has epilepsy. Nonetheless, the germ theory of disease is still unknown to Jesus, which seems odd that the Son of the Creator, or God himself, be unaware of dangerous microscopic organisms. (Imagine how many lives Jesus would have saved in child birth alone, from year one through to the 19th century, if he had of let us in on that little health secret?) The woman pleads with Jesus that he exorcise the demon or demons within her daughter. Jesus replies coldly, "Piss off, you're not a Jew". The woman sobs uncontrollably and her desperate pleas become more vocal. Jesus shouts;

"I was sent only to the lost sheep of the nation of Israel."
(Matthew 15:24)

The woman cries in further desperation. Jesus looks at her scornfully, and says:

"It is not good to take the children's bread and throw it to the dogs." (Matthew 15:27)

Anyone familiar with Middle Eastern culture will tell you that to refer to any person or persons as a dog, is as low an insult as any individual can hurl at another. Why? Dogs eat carrion and scraps, defecate, urinate and mate etc with no inhibitions. Henceforth, they were associated with being bad mannered, of low moral integrity, and having no honor. What Jesus, in effect, was saying, "Piss off, you sub-human thing, you".

Sure, you can accuse me of over dramatization all you want, but this is the essence of his message. He's made it clear in this dialogue that he is concerned for Jews only, as was his nation's psyche at the time, and anyone unfortunate, in his eyes, not to have been born a descendent of Jacob is unworthy of the scraps from his table. This is a damning passage - make no mistake about it. This is racist Jesus in full flight!

If we are to examine the historical Jesus then we must see him only as a Rabbi that put his own spin or flavor on the Jewish law or Bible. He saw himself as conduit to bring his people, the Jews, back in step with not only the law but with God too, this is, if you've read the Old Testament, an overarching theme (i.e. prophets coming to return the 12 tribes to their Law, their Lore and their God).

Moreover, if we look at the principle tenets of the Christian faith it is this: Those that believe that Jesus was the Son of God, who died on the cross to atone for all of our past and future sins, will experience everlasting life in the kingdom of Heaven. This is not something Jesus ever said. Jesus' position was clear, heaven would be reserved exclusively for the '"righteous." In other words, he was referring to those that obeyed God's law to the letter. The doctrine of salvation through belief in Jesus comes from the marketing whizz huckster Saint Paul in his letter to the newly established Church in Rome in approximately 60 AD:

> *"Therefore no-one will be declared righteous in his sight by observing the law; rather, through the law we become conscious of sin... This righteousness from God comes to those who believe." (Romans 3:20-22 NIV)*

> *"That if you confess with your mouth, 'Jesus is Lord,' and believe in your heart that God raised him from the dead, you will be saved." (Romans 10:9 NIV)*

Paul outlines that salvation comes through believing only in Jesus' death and resurrection, and therefore in one whoosh of the pen completely overturned what Jesus had to say about the importance of observing the law to the letter. In another verse, Paul even makes the claim that observing the law will only hinder one's prospects of obtaining the magical VIP pass into heaven when he writes:

> *"We who are Jews by birth and not 'Gentile sinners' know that a man is not justified by observing the law, but by faith in Jesus Christ. So we, too, have put our faith in Christ Jesus that we may be justified by faith in Christ and not by observing the law, because by observing the law no one will be justified." (Galatians 2:15)*

Nowhere in the New Testament does Jesus make any statement regarding the supposedly sacrificial purpose behind his death. It is Paul, and the Gospels that give their differing reasons for Jesus' crucifixion. Paul says he died for our sins. Luke says it was to make the Jews realize they are sinful and therefore need to turn to God for forgiveness. Mark says it is an atoning sacrifice for the original sin. Don't be confused, atonement and forgiveness are two different things, but we will tackle that in a later chapter.

The point is, these respective philosophies and theologies concerning the death of Jesus-the-Jew, which form the central tenet for the Christian religion, are built on commentary not only external to Jesus and foreign to his beliefs, but by people that never actually met him. Not only had these authors never met the guy, but also, Jesus had been dead for some time before they'd even been born. Furthermore, with no written testament from Jesus' own hand, anything the Gospel writers penned was their own conjecture based on lore.

Christianity was, therefore, never established on the words of Jesus but rather the writings of others, most of whom are unknown to us, all of whom never heard Jesus speak a solitary word. Effectively, all these authors had accomplished was to learn of the fanciful fairy-tales about this man named Jesus and then so extrapolated on them to their own ends.

At this point, I feel compelled to point out that I am giving just a broad brush over the origins of Christianity. Much of this book concerns the Gospels and Paul, and for now we will skip ahead to how this religion came into prominence and ultimately western civilization's consciousness.

Where do we begin? Well, first of all it would be an understatement to say that it began with humble beginnings. In fact, that would be an overstatement. For the first three centuries after the death of Jesus, those that called themselves Christians numbered less than 40,000 throughout the Roman Empire. Considering that the Jewish population at that time is estimated to have been approximately 4,000,000 people. This places the Christian total at, give or take, 1% of their Jewish counterparts. This amounts to little more than a fringe minority. Even today's Scientologists have greater market share, and those guys are freaking crazy. (I've intentionally misspelled crazy to give the adjective added emphasis ie Mel Gibson is crazy)

Moreover, the Christian belief system seemed so whacky and absurd to Jews, and non-Jews alike that the early believers were routinely arrested for insanity and fed to the lions as sport. Karen Armstrong in her book *A History of God* writes:

"Christianity, therefore, had the worst of both worlds. It lacked the venerable antiquity of Judaism and had none of the attractive rituals of paganism, which everybody could see and appreciate. It was also a potential threat, since Christians insisted that theirs was the only God and that all the other deities were delusions."

The educated class of Rome and Athens looked to philosophy rather than religion when it came to the search for enlightenment. With the intelligencia finding personal comfort in the teachings of Plato and Socrates, these same educated individuals regarded the God of Abraham as a ferocious, barbaric, and primitive deity... which isn't that big a stretch, considering that the God of the Old Testament is all of those things and more.

Moreover, the Christian belief that a god could suffer a gruesome, disgraceful death on a dirty, dusty, isolated and obscure corner of the Roman Empire seemed beyond the pale of rationality for most first century thinkers. Ultimately, from a Roman perspective, Christianity seemed neither a religion nor a philosophy, and accordingly it was shunned as CRAZY! (Cap locks to denote crazier than Mel Gibson CRAZY) Imagine that...

What set Christianity apart from other religions of the time, though, was its desperate need to convert others to its faith. The early martyrs of the Church, Saint Paul, Saint Peter, and Saint Valentine were all beheaded, and went to their deaths willingly for their religious belief. This fact puzzled Romans in particular, who believed blood sacrifice to be the archaic machinations of a socially retarded ancient civilization. Martin Goodman, author *Rome & Jerusalem*, writes:

"This sense of mission set Christians apart from other religious groups, including Jews, in the early Roman Empire. The notion that it is desirable for existing enthusiasts to encourage outsiders to worship the god to whom they are devoted was not obvious in the ancient world. Adherents of particular cults did not generally judge the power of divinity by the number of congregants prepared to bring offerings or attend festivals. On the contrary, it was common for pagans to take pride in the local nature of their religious lives, establishing a special relationship between themselves and the god of a family or place, without wishing, let alone expecting, others to join in worshipping the same god. Christians in the first generation were different, espousing a proselytizing mission which was a shocking novelty in the ancient world."

Further to the above, the fledgling religion's claims of miracles elicited great ridicule from the intellectual communities of Athens, and Rome, and we have evidence of this. Evidence that confirms the tenets of the Christian faith seemed preposterously absurd to anyone with a triple figure IQ, even way back then.

One such source comes from a book titled *The True Word* published in the late second century by a man named Celsus. The author argued that Christianity was a foolish and dangerous religion reserved for ignorant lower-class people. While we don't have a copy of *The True Word* itself, we do have, interestingly, a retort to the charges made by Celsus from one of the Church's founding fathers, Origen. Comically, to me at least, is that Origen doesn't deny the allegation that Christianity is a religion reserved for dimwits. In his book titled *Against Celsus*:

*"The Christians' injunctions are like this. "**Let no one educated**, no one wise, no one sensible draw near. **For these abilities are thought by us to be evils**. But as for*

*anyone ignorant, anyone stupid, anyone uneducated,
anyone who is a child, let him come boldly."*

*"In private houses also we see wool-workers, cobblers,
laundry-workers, and the most illiterate and bucolic
yokels, who would not dare to say anything at all in front
of their elders and more intelligent masters. But whenever
they get hold of children in private and some **stupid
women** with them, they let out some astonishing
statements, as, for example, that they must not pay any
attention to their father and school teachers; they say that
these talk nonsense and have no understanding. But if
they like, they should leave father and their schoolmasters,
and go along with the women and little children who are
their playfellows to the wooldressers' shop, or to the
cobbler's or the washerwoman's shop, that they learn
perfection. And by saying this they persuade them."*

By the very early stages of the fourth century, Christianity
was still somewhat of an underworld religion, spoken
about in small gatherings in the back of various
sympathizers' homes scattered throughout the
Mediterranean. Its followers treated like criminals at
worst, or social lepers at best, and Justin Bieber fans
somewhere in the middle. A vast majority of the early
Christians were former pagan multi-god worshippers,
such as God of the Moon, God of the Sun, and so forth.
Effectively, anything to do with agriculture had a god.
These Greeks, Macedonian, and Roman farmers would
hear stories of this guy called Jesus, long after he had died.
And I will use Bart D Ehrmans', author of *Jesus Interrupted*,
words to illustrate the amazing phenomenon that was the
beginning of Christianity:

*"I am a coppersmith who lives in Ephesus, in Asia Minor.
A stranger comes to my town and begins to preach about
the miraculous life and death of Jesus. I hear all the stories
he has to tell, and decide to give up my devotion to the
local pagan divinity, Athena, and become a follower of the*

Jewish God and Jesus his son. I then convert my wife, based on the stories that I repeat. She tells the next-door neighbor, and she converts. This neighbor tells the stories to her husband, a merchant, and he converts. He goes on a business trip to the city of Smyrna and he tells his business associate the stories. He converts, and then tells his wife, who also converts.

This woman who has now converted has heard all sorts of stories about Jesus. And from whom? One of the apostles? No, from her husband. Well, whom did he hear it from? His next door neighbor, the merchant of Ephesus. Where did he hear them? His wife. And she? My wife. And she? From me. And where did I hear it from? An eyewitness? No, I heard it from the stranger who came to town. This is how Christianity spread, year after year, decade after decade, until eventually someone wrote down the stories. What do you suppose happened to the stories over the years, as they were told and retold, not as disinterested news stories reported by eyewitnesses but as propaganda meant to convert people to faith."

Ehrman succinctly describes the method for conversion and recruitment of early Christians. The method accounted for little more than the spreading of hearsay and anecdotes. And for a point of reference let us not forget that hearsay is inadmissible as evidence in a Court of Law today. This really does give one a sense of how and why the new religion struggled for relevancy for the first few hundred years after the death of its star, Jesus. Now, there is a natural tendency to dismiss three or four hundred years as a day or two when reflecting on ancient history, due, in part, to the fact that we often speak of thousands of years. To put into some modern day context, however, if Jesus' death took place during the War of American Independence - we would still, today, be unaware of anyone by his name. Humble beginnings indeed!

Christianity's big break, however, came in the fourth century. In the midst of Christians still being thrown to live animals as a form of sport, one man's conversion changed everything, and I do mean everything. His conversion, the reason there is a Church in every freaking neighborhood, a Bible in your house, and 'In God We Trust' emblazoned on the hard earned dollars in your pocket. His name – the Roman Emperor Constantine.

The Roman Empire, by the fourth century, was beginning to collapse in on itself; the cracks in the wallpaper were evident to the elite and plainly obvious to Constantine. He needed a device that could bring unity to his crumbling Empire. An empire that stretched to the most northern parts of Europe, to the edge of Asia, and down into the African continent.

With so many varying societies and cultures under his direct control, and with their respective myriad religions and gods, Constantine, under advisement from societal elite, believed a one-god religion could bring stability and uniformity to his empire. However, in the shopping aisles for a one-god (monotheistic) religion, there were only Judaism or Christianity to choose from. The Romans thought the Jewish religion to be far too strict and in many instances barbaric, thus Constantine knew the people would too quickly reject this offer. Christianity, on the other hand, required little interruption in the personal lives of its followers.

You weren't required to circumcise yourself, slaughter animals as offerings, or even attend a Temple for group worship. Constantine had a read through some of Saint Paul's letters and thought to himself, "this is a religion one can follow from the comfort of one's own bathhouse." This partly explains its popularity in the United States, a religion you can follow without so much as changing the television channel... let alone following any of the central principles.

His decision to convert had begun. But first he needed a convincing story to tell his minnows. No Roman worth his linen toga was going to commence praising the memory of a dead Jew in any great hurry without a sensational marketing campaign to provide a little 'credibility'. Constantine, after careful strategizing, hatched his plan, and he sold it heroically.

The Emperor was leading his troops into war at the Battle of Milvian Bridge in 312 AD In the heat of battle, with the Romans looking anything but assured of victory, it is said that Constantine had his epiphany. As swords struck flesh and metal all around him, the Emperor averted his eyes skyward and at that very moment he saw a cross of light above the sun with the Greek words 'Εν Τουτω Νικα". Translated into English, this means 'by this, conquer!'

Later that night, as his troops rested in preparation for the next day's fighting he told his generals of what he had seen, and he commanded his entire army to adorn their shields with the Christian symbol, the cross. You don't need to be a scriptwriter to guess what happened next. That's right, the Romans gave the opposition a royal ass whipping with good ole Jesus on their side, riding shotgun. Now, before you say Jesus was a divine friend of the Romans lest we forget that the Roman Empire collapsed completely, not long after. Some celestial friend, huh? I can't help but wonder how things may have turned out differently had the Romans stuck with Jupiter (the Roman version of Zeus) as their god.

Constantine's conversion was made official by way of a public baptism, and the following year he endorsed the Edict of Milan, which declared religious freedom for Christians, putting an end to their illegitimacy. The crucifix was no longer a symbol of organized crime. They were no longer the ugly, unwanted bastard children of religious faith. Christians could now teach and preach the story of Jesus without the fear of imprisonment or death.

With carte blanche to recruit and convert, and with the Emperor's sponsorship, mass conversions throughout Europe and Asia-Minor began. Conversions were not effected with miraculous signs or answered prayers. Rather, pagans were converted either by evangelic stories or promises, or did so for political gain. More often than not, staring down the tip of a sword.

Competing religions, including paganism and Judaism were not proselytizing faiths. Typically, you were either born a Jew or you weren't. Your parents worshipped the planetary gods, or you didn't. This was not the case for Christianity, however:

> *"Judaism spread primarily through migration and procreation. Proselytizing mission was, on the other hand, crucial to the spread of Christianity. The early Christians, moreover, did not have a central cultic, economic and political institution comparable to the Temple in Jerusalem, which attracted outsiders."*
> *[Esler, Modelling Early Christianity (Routledge):129]*

Christianity shortly thereafter became the official religion of the Roman Empire, and the rest they say is history.

The next step, however, in institutionalizing the fledgling religion would be just as problematic. They now had to develop a Holy Book, set apart from, but complimentary to the Hebrew Bible. Constantine commissioned a meeting of church figureheads and theologians, the Nicaea Council, to pull together as many as possible of the hundreds or thousands of manuscripts that were floating about which told of Jesus or his teachings.

There were dozens of Paul's letters to the early Christians in the first century that needed to be vetted; many of his Epistles were excluded. There were biographical accounts of Jesus from unknown sources such as the Gospels of Matthew, Mark, Luke, and John. There were also the Book of Judith, the Book of Baruch, the Epistle of Jeremy, the History of Susanna, the First and

Second Gospels of Infancy of Jesus Christ, the Epistle of Barnabas, the Gospel according to the Egyptians, the Apocalypse of Peter, Acts of Paul, the Shepherd of Hermas, the Infancy Gospels of Thomas, the Gnostic Gospels and a galactic shitload more – to all be considered for a place in history… in the Bible.

What was the central objective of the council? Simply, to select texts that were the most complimentary to the Jesus story, which they felt would best support their view of how to take the religion forward. In other words, writings that made him appear most divine, and were the least contradictory in nature, which in the end they didn't do all that well, despite much deliberation.

One of the first to be binned was the Infancy Gospels of Thomas, for example. This was mainly due to the illustrations of a child Jesus who messed around with his kick-ass magical powers in much the same way a young Harry Potter may have. One such story includes a young Jesus transforming his playmates into goats, or making real life sparrows from mud. Another story from Thomas was Jesus bringing his playmate back to life, after he had fallen off the roof they were playing on, in order to clear the child Jesus from killing his young friend… that's right, he only brought his friend back to absolve himself of a murder charge… some guy, that Jesus, some guy!

Other Gospels omitted included that of Barnabas, Mary, and Judas amongst others. But in went Matthew, Mark, Luke, and John. And the Bible was created; a collection of books sanctioned by a bunch of old white men with questionable motives. This often comes as another surprise to Christians who believe that the Bible descended from Heaven the day after Jesus died. It really is a very human book written by humans, and deliberated upon by later humans.

Now, don't be thinking the Council of Nicaea had just a session or two to deliberate on the inclusion and exclusion of what should and shouldn't be included in the New Testament. These debates waged on for centuries, before consensus was reached amongst the founding fathers of the church.

There were bitter arguments over the issue of Jesus' divinity, to name just one such example. You had one side arguing for Jesus being merely a human that preached a new-age version of God's law. You had another side argue that Jesus was God himself. Further, many regarded Matthew and Luke's claim of a virgin birth and resurrection to be ludicrous. Imagine that? The idea of spontaneous pregnancy in an otherwise virgin teen and the ascension into a mythical afterlife post crucifixion was regarded as ludicrous? Wow, what a surprise!

The single most important debate put before the Council, however, became known as the Arian controversy. How contentious was this so-called controversy? Let's just say had resolution not been reached, Constantine would have tossed Christianity into the too hard basket, and we'd most likely today know as much about this religion as we do about Rastafarianism. And no, just because you own Bob Marley's Greatest Hits, smoke ganja, and wear a tea cozy on your head, does not make you a Rasta, mon.

The controversy began as a small argument between a bishop by the name Alexander and a priest known as Arius. It was Arius the shit-stirrer that first proposed the idea that if the Father (God) begat the Son (Jesus), Jesus must have had a beginning. In other words, there had to have been a time when Jesus was not, and that his substance was from nothing like the rest of creation. Arius had his argument well grounded in scripture, citing examples where Jesus had said specifically that the Father was greater than he. Arius wrote a letter to Bishop Alexander that read:

"God was the only begotten, the only eternal, the only one without beginning, the only true, the only one who has immortality, the only wise, the only good, the only potentate."

Arius pointed to many passages from the Bible to back his claim that Jesus and God were not one and the same, including the following verse from Proverbs that describes the divine wisdom:

"Through him all things came to be, not one thing had its being but through him."

The fact that Jesus never once called himself God, outside of the I'm as high as a kite gospel of John, and repeatedly referred to God as his "Father" implied the distinction, and thus Arius argued what would appeared to be a no-brainer. But the theological powers at be thought otherwise, and ultimately the end of this story illustrates just how arbitrarily man made this religion, as is the case of all religions, truly is.

It was Arius theological assertion that the heavenly afterlife had been made possible for mankind because Jesus had paved the way for us. He was a man that lived a perfect life; he obeyed all of God's laws; and his death and resurrection erased our supposed debt of sin. If we followed in Jesus' footsteps then the afterlife was made possible for us too. This is the way Arius interpreted the scriptures.

But the Bishop of Alexander, and his assistant Athanasius had a more pessimistic view of mankind's ability for good. According to both men, salvation is made impossible if only Jesus were a man of flesh, and not God himself. In other words, only he who created the world had the ability or right to save it.

The Council of Nicaea, however, condemned the views of Arius, and in doing so published its creed proclaiming

that the "Son" was "one in being with the Father" by use
of the Greek word "homoousius".

"We believe in God, the Father Almighty,
maker of all things, visible and invisible,
and in one Lord, Jesus Christ,
the Son of God,
the only begotten of the Father,
that is, of the substance (ousia) of the Father,
God from God,
light from light,
true God from true God,
begotten not made,
of one substance (homoousian) with the Father,
through whom all things are made,
those things that are in heaven and
those things that are on earth,
who for us men and for our salvation
came down and was made man,
suffered,
rose again on the third day, ascended into heaven
and will come
to judge the living and the dead.
And we believe in the Holy Spirit."

More than three hundred bishops, from all parts of the
Empire, attended the Nicea Council. These men were the
early 'street-fighters' for Christianity. They were often
threatened with abduction or death because of what many
outsiders viewed as a radical faith. This persecution
molded the founding fathers into dogged, determined and
ambitious builders of the fledgling religion. Thus they
were extremely sensitive to non-conforming beliefs or
views that, they feared, could roadblock or divert their
naïve and idealistic objectives.

This Arian controversy had the potential to derail the
regime before it started, and this is why the defining of

Jesus and God as one and the same or as different entities - was agenda item number one for the Council.

Item number two - the hotly debated question of what day to celebrate the resurrection.

Eventually, all but seventeen of the three hundred Bishops signed the creed that included the wording "homoousias", meaning that God and the Son were one and the same. But the seventeen that sided with Arius threatened to drag this inside bickering and politicking out into the cobbled streets of Rome, which would have certainly put an end to the burgeoning faith. Analogically, they say there are three things you never want to see created before your very eyes: laws, sausages, and religions.

The Emperor Constantine was greatly agitated by the boorish and semantic controversy, so he sent a letter to Arius and Alexander in an attempt to persuade he and the 'gang of seventeen' to get their shit together and lay aside their differences. He wrote:

> "This contention has not arisen respecting any important command of the law, nor has any new opinion been introduced with regard to the worship of God; but you both entertain the same sentiments, so that you may join in one communion. It is thought to be not only indecorous, but altogether unlawful, that so numerous a people of God should be governed and directed at your pleasure, while you are thus emulously contending with each other, and quarrelling about small and very trifling matters."

It's odd that the Emperor would regard the identity or character of Christ as a "trifling matter", then again, Constantine was obviously using Christianity to his own political needs. This much is clear. Nevertheless, Constantine's words were adequate and ultimately reassured Arius enough to soften his objection, and the doctrine of the Trinity became the fairy-tale bullshit orthodoxy that we all know and love today.

The father, the son, and the Holy Spirit were now one and the same. This non-Biblical referenced doctrine created by the Church caused at least one Rabbi, David Kimhi, to laugh like a Bavarian whore, high on nitrous oxide, when he quipped:

"Therefore, with reference to this God whom you call Father, Son, and Holy Spirit, that part which you call Father must be prior to that which you call Son, for if they were always coexistent, they would have to be called twin brothers."

Moreover, if the Son is the Father – what of Mary getting pregnant? Is this not an incestuous congregation? The father has sex with the mother in order to conceive the son who is also the father... so technically the son, who is also the father, had sex with his mother... Oedipus, anyone? Freud would have had a field day with this faux family!

In regards to other theological differences, the majority view consensus became orthodoxy, while the rest became heretical scripture that was eventually capped in the ass by the Church.

The definition of what it meant to be a Christian became defined as:

"I believe in God the Father, the Creator of Heaven and Earth, and in Jesus Christ his Son, born of the Virgin Mary, who suffered under Pontius Pilate, was crucified, dead and buried. He arose on the third day and ascended into Heaven where he sits at the right hand of God the Father, from whence he shall come to judge the quick and the dead. I believe in the Holy Ghost, the Holy Catholic Church (universal), and in life everlasting."

Christianity as we know it today had begun. God damn it!

CHAPTER THREE

Who Wrote
The New Testament?

In what I hope is not a spoiler alert, we did not wake up with a copy of the New Testament on our doorstep the moment Jesus' ghostly ass ascended into heaven, even though it was obviously already there, because God was Jesus, apparently. Confused?

Further, Jesus himself wrote not a single word of the New Testament. Not a single poem, much less an op-ed article on why upon reflection killing your daughter for backchat is probably not a great idea.

Christopher Hitchens believes that the best argument against a historical Jesus is the fact that none of his disciples left us with a single record or document regarding Jesus or his teachings. All we have is a whole bunch of campfire stories from people who weren't born for generations after Jesus' supposed crucifixion... or cruci-fiction – see what I did there? I digress.

Numerous men with their own theological motives wrote the New Testament. So, who were these men we doth speak of? Who was Paul? Who were the Gospels? Short answer: with the exclusion of Paul, we don't know. We have no idea as to the identity of Matthew, Mark, Luke, or John. So, what do we know? Well, we know a lot, and what we do know is hardly complimentary to the Church or the historical legitimacy of the Christian faith.

The New Testament is a collection of writings, twenty seven in total, of which twelve are credited to the authorship of Paul, five to the Gospels (whoever wrote Luke also wrote Acts), and the balance remain open for debate i.e. author unknown.

Further convoluting the problem of authorship, is the fact modern scholars are in unison that a number of the letters credited to Paul were in fact forgeries i.e. written by others claiming to be Paul, in particular, the books of Timothy and Thessalonians.

What often comes as a shock to your Sunday wine and cracker Christian is that neither the Gospels, nor Paul, ever met Jesus the man himself. Moreover, none of the Gospels met the people that met the people that met Jesus. Thus, we have not a single eyewitness record of the life and death of Jesus H Christ. In fact, we have not a single self-written manuscript, birth or death certificate, or even a solitary independent unbiased eyewitness record of the most famous man to have ever graced western civilization.

What did Greek or Roman sources write about Jesus during the periods 1 AD to 100 AD? The answer is a short one: NOTHING! We know more about the Roman Senator Cicero, who lived during the same era, than we do of the acclaimed Son of God. Jesus, in my mind, is much like the comic hero the Phantom – the ghost who walked.

The fact that the Gospels and Paul were not eyewitnesses to Jesus' life is not an issue in contention. It's just a simple fact! Moreover, neither the Gospels nor Paul make any claims as to have ever seeing or meeting Jesus. This one little point should trouble any Christian to the point of disbelief as LITERALLY NOTHING IN THE BIBLE CAN BE DIRECTLY, VERIFIABLY, ATTRIBUTED TO JESUS!

In effect, we have only hearsay, which is based upon more hearsay, which is based upon more hearsay still, which is again based on more hearsay. And as we discussed earlier, we know hearsay to be testimony unworthy of consideration in a court of law. The question is, for a believer, is hearsay upon hearsay upon hearsay sufficient enough a foundation for your religious belief?

Dan Barker, a former evangelical minister cum atheist, writes in his book '*Losing Faith in Faith*':

> *"There is not a single contemporary historical mention of Jesus, not by Romans or by Jews, not by believers or by unbelievers, not during his entire lifetime. This does not disprove his existence, but it certainly casts great doubt on the historicity of a man who was supposedly widely known to have made a great impact on the world. Someone should have noticed."*

Based on a lack of external evidence, eyewitness testimony, conflicting Gospel accounts, and an absence of independent records – the only thing we know about Jesus, with any degree of certainty is the following:

- He was a Palestinian Jew
- He was raised in Galilee
- He spent most of his life in that immediate area. A rural area, outside of the more 'sophisticated' Jerusalem, that practiced a primitive form of Judaism.
- Jewish parents raised him.
- He was circumcised as a Jew.
- He observed all the Jewish holidays, and ceremonies, even the ones like the 'Festival of The Lights' that had not been invented for some 150 years after his death... so much for Gospel inerrancy!
- He lived and taught as a pious God-fearing Jew.

Outside of the above points, the remainder, we can be sure, are myths tagged onto his biography decades, and centuries after he had passed. Tales designed to extract religious meaning from Jesus' life and teachings. We know this by examining the New Testament, in particular the irreconcilable contradictions between the Gospels' writings, as we will in great detail.

Martin Goodman, in his book *Rome & Jerusalem*, examines the spread of Christian influence through the Roman Empire, writes:

> *"Jesus lived and died in Galilee and Judaea in the first half of the first century CE. That this fact is one of the few which can be asserted with any certainty about the founding figure of the Christian Church is the result not of a paucity of ancient stories about Jesus but of contradictions between multifarious tales which abounded among his followers in the two centuries after his death, as they tried to extract religious meaning from his life and teachings. The story of a remarkable individual put to death in Jerusalem but retaining great power and resurrection was elaborated and altered by the pious over succeeding generations."*

What do we know of the respective Gospel identities? Well, we know they were highly educated Greek speaking authors. Who were Jesus' disciples? They were peasant class, illiterate, Aramaic speaking goat herders and fishermen. At the start of the first century, it is estimated that less than 10% of the Roman Empire could read or write, and the vast majority of those that could, could do so only at a very rudimentary level i.e. the extent of their ability was to pen 'my name is Bob' and 'damn, that Cleopatra chick is hot'.

The skill of reading and writing was a privilege of the wealthy elite, the upper classes, who had the resources to pay for an education. They also had plenty of time up their sleeves, as their every whim was taken care of by their slaves. Furthermore, aside from clearly not being of the underclass, which Jesus was said to have attracted, the Gospel authors were as ignorant of Palestinian geography as they were of Jewish customs. Therefore, it is most likely that the Gospels wrote about Jesus on the back porch of their respective Athens or Roman villas as they enjoyed a selection of the very finest Tuscan wines.

If we recall Chapter one, we discussed how the stories of Jesus passed by word of mouth in its early days, using Bart D Ehrman's illustration of a 'word of mouth religion' of fairytales and myths. From there, what we have in the four Gospels, are four guys that started to put these campfire stories of mythology and lore to paper.

Presumably, Mark, whoever he was, heard the verbal story of how Jesus healed a man with leprosy, became suitably impressed then wrote about it. He started collecting all of these fanciful stories along the way until he had what he regarded as a complete picture of who Jesus was.

The question now is; did Matthew and Luke write down the stories, in the same manner as Mark, which they heard around the campfire while toasting marshmallows? If the answer is yes, then you are getting close to having three independent records of Jesus' life, notwithstanding the fact that their stories would still be based on little more than hearsay. Unfortunately for Christianity, however, the answer is a resounding NO! Matthew and Luke did not write independent of Mark, they in fact copied from Mark, but then added stories and verses to suit their own motives, theology, tradition and respective culture.

The Gospel of Mark was written more or less in 70 AD, thirty-five years after Jesus' death. Many years later Matthew and Luke plagiarized from Mark, added their own spin with some additional external sources, which scholars identify respectively as 'Q' (Matthew) and 'L' (Luke), thrown in for good measure. Thus, Matthew, Mark and Luke are called the 'Synoptic Gospels'. Synoptic meaning 'seeing together' or with the same eye.

John, however, just shoots from the hip and distances himself from the other three in so many theological ways. He goes as far as to say that Jesus is God, which is ultimately why John has become the favorite Gospel for conservative nut-bag Christians today. Yes, I'm looking at you John 3:16 sign carrying guy. Many of the most revered and most celebrated stories are unique to John i.e. the woman taken into adultery, the raising of Lazarus, the seven signs, the water into wine, and the healing of a man born blind. Such gratuity, such embellishment, such fairytale hopefulness!

Essentially, the biographical picture of Jesus is drawn from, in the most, Mark's gospel, who merely recorded the things he heard about Jesus. As an exercise you should read the Gospel of Mark aloud using a stopwatch to time your effort. What you will discover is this: you can, more or less, read the entire book in less than two hours. That's it! A two-hour monologue of the most famous man in history is, effectively, all that we have.

While Matthew and Luke add their own respective 'flavor' (which actually tastes a lot like an evening of bad decisions), often giving varying reasons for events with added mythology on top of Mark's stories, the similarities remain obvious even to a casual reader. In my first book, *God Hates You, Hate Him Back*, I showed the main stories of the four Gospels side by side, providing the reader with a comparative analysis and birds-eye view.

John's gospel, however, is its own unique barrel of monkeys! A majority of the stories found in the Gospel of John are not found in the other three, and likewise, the stories found in Matthew, Mark, and Luke are not found in John. Effectively, all four Gospels do their best, with a rear view mirror, to make things appear in harmony. Which I'm sure would have worked if humanity had stayed the rabble of poor cretins who were satisfied by the apparent 'truthiness' of the stories in the first place.

In regards to this, I do enjoy Christopher Hitchen's snarky take:

> *"...just like the Old Testament, the 'New' one is also a work of crude carpentry, hammered together long after its purported events, and full of improvised attempts to make things come out right."*

As we will review in later chapters, the variances in content are stark, and the discrepancies breathtaking. Furthermore, Paul makes very little mention of Jesus' life, as he concerns himself mostly on the death and resurrection; what Jesus' death means; and preparation for the second coming.

Originals Lost

The thorns in the side of faith don't stop here, however. Further muddying the waters is the fact we do not have any of the original manuscripts of the Bible. The originals are lost. We don't know when and we don't know by whom. What we have are copies of the copies. In some instances, the copies we have are twentieth generation copies. We have to bear in mind that 2,000 years ago there were no Kinkos, mass media, book publishers, or printing press. If someone wrote a book there'd only be one copy. That is until someone else thought the book was worth a read and they'd, in turn, make their own copy. Let me illustrate.

Let's say, for example, that in 100 AD I wrote a book titled *How to Make Love like Tiger Woods.* My neighbor sees my book resting on the coffee table and decides that he too would like to get on the Tiger program and asks if he can have a copy. I oblige, but the question becomes - how do we make a copy with no printers, as was the case with Rome 1,900 years ago?

The only way is for him to make a hand written copy of my book, the original. Subsequently, for the next two months my neighbor spends his evenings writing his copy of my book. BUT do you think his copy will be identical to mine? Well, most likely not. He may not think the chapter titled *'Don't Give Your Home Phone Number to Randoms'* to be relevant to his situation, thus he omits that. He may also not be comfortable with my liberal use of the word 'fuck', because I am known to use 'fuck' as a punctuation mark.

Thus, he omits all the fucks. And a few other changes here and a few changes there, and maybe the addition of one or two of his own chapters. So, now we have two copies of *How to Make Love Like Tiger*. But while being similar the two are far from being identical.

We move on. Let's say my neighbor's boss wants to improve his success rate away from home, like Tiger. He now makes a copy of my neighbor's copy, his copy a variation of my original. With his omissions here, and his own additions there, we now have three copies all unalike or unique in their own way. And it goes on and goes on and goes on.

Despite my fifth grade sense of humor, or lack thereof, this is an excellent illustration of how we came to possess the copies that we have some 2,000 years down the track. This understanding really foils the claim that the Bible is the word of God. How can it be so when we don't really have any bloody idea what the original word of God was?

The wonderful HL Mencken writes in his book The Treatise on the Gods:

> *"The simple fact is that the New Testament, as we know it, is a helter-skelter accumulation of more or less discordant documents, some of them probably of respectable origin but others palpably apocryphal, and that most of them, the good along with the bad, show unmistakable signs of having being tampered with."*

The King James Bible

Nothing supports Mencken's assertion better than the story of how it is that we have the King James Version (KJV) of the Bible. The KJV was compiled only 400 years ago in 1611, a full fifteen hundred years after the Gospels and Paul had penned their respective original works. Despite a Texas Governor's loopy quip during a Gubernatorial debate, the original manuscripts of the Bible were not written in English. They weren't, just trust me on this!

The New Testament manuscripts were written in Greek but the very first published edition of the Greek New Testament was not produced until 1522. Some crazy Dutch dude by the name of Erasmus took seven years to compile *Edito Princeps*, meaning first published edition. It is from Erasmus writings that the writers/translators of the King James Version used to pen what many American fundamentalist Christians believe is the inerrant word of God.

Now, here's where it gets shaky. Where did Erasmus get his manuscript copies of the gospels and epistles? Did they fall from heaven? Of course they didn't. The simple truth, the clog wearing Erasmus threw both legs over the back of his pony and galloped to Basel, Switzerland, the land of dark chocolate, the home of Roman Polanski, and even darker porn.

Anyway, when Erasmus got to the Swiss city did he find a treasure trove of original manuscripts? No, he didn't. What he got there was just a bunch of medieval versions. As matter of fact, he copied from a 12th century copy of the gospels. Do you have any idea how many copies of copies and how many sets of scribes' hands the translations got polluted by before the guy who wrote his copy in the 12th century? The mind boggles.

Further, the version of the gospels that Erasmus used contained the respective stories of the woman taken in adultery ('Cast the first stone') in John, and the last twelve verses of Mark. These passages were never originally included in the gospels. In other words, these were stories added on down the line by anonymous writers with their own theological, traditional and cultural motives.

Once again, the above is not a contentious issue as Biblical scholars are unanimously in agreement that the original New Testament manuscripts are lost to us. Your pastor that was a former drug addict or used car salesman, who now preaches the 'Good Word' to you on Sunday's in between choruses of uber cool (but seriously gay) Christian rock music may tell you otherwise, but he's wrong. And ignorant. And ugly. Also, he's sleeping with your wife.

A majority of church leaders are not trained in textual criticism, let alone understand the authenticity issues as they relate to manuscript transmission. Hell, even Wikipedia makes the following statement:

> "In attempting to determine the original text of the New Testament books, some modern textual critics have identified sections as probably not original. In modern translations of the Bible, the results of textual criticism have led to certain verses being left out or marked as not original. These possible later additions include the following:
>
> -The ending of Mark
>
> -The story in John of the woman taken in adultery, Most bibles have footnotes to indicate areas that have disputed source documents. Bible commentaries also discuss these, sometimes in great detail."

The variances amongst the copies; that is, the evidently obvious changes - both big and small - that were made to the Jesus narrative troubled the founding fathers of the Church, so much so that Origen once complained:

> "The differences among the manuscripts have become great, either through the negligence of some copyists or through the perverse audacity of others; they either neglect to check over what they have transcribed, or, in the process of checking, they make additions or deletions as they please."

This is a breathtaking admission from the early Church. Admirable but not as humorous as Origen's retort to Celsus:

> "Some believers, as though from a drinking bout, go so far as to oppose themselves and alter the original text of the

gospel three or four or several times over, and they change its characters to enable them to deny difficulties in face of criticism."

There you have it in black and white, my peeps. Not only are the respective third hand accounts of Jesus tampered with, but we've also discovered that this religion was started for the simpletons of the Roman Empire - for the purpose of reunification (control). A kind of theology for dummies, if you will. Sure, some smart people joined the ranks along the way such as Augustine and Aquinos, who, by the way, demanded all heretics be burnt to a stake. But it would appear the lure of an afterlife is a hard offer to resist no matter how high your intelligence quotient. It was on this promise that Christianity began to flourish.

CHAPTER FOUR

The Gospels on Jesus' Birth

What Christians Know

Ask any Christian to narrate the birth of Jesus and they will describe for you the nativity scene we know oh so well at Christmas time. Displayed in churches, homes, shopping malls, and even the White House exhibits an eighteenth century Italian version of the nativity during the Christmas season.

The nativity scene typically portrays three wise men (the magi) led by a star to baby Jesus, who is found in a manger. The magi come bearing gifts for the child prodigy, namely frankincense, gold, and myrrh. Were it me, I would have been really pissed that they didn't all bring gold. I mean, who the hell wants bloody frankincense? And what the fuck is Myrrh?

With God's first family gathered around baby Jesus wrapped snuggly in his blankey; the magi, the angels, and the stable animals look upon the messiah in adoration.

The Joke

Q: What would have happened if it had been Three Wise Women instead of the Three Wise Men?

A: They would have:
- Asked directions
- Arrived on time
- Helped deliver the baby
- Cleaned the stable
- Made a casserole, and
- Brought practical gifts

But then, what would they have said when they left...?

- "Did you see the sandals Mary was wearing with that gown?"
- "That baby didn't look anything like Joseph."
- "Can you believe they'd let all those disgusting animals in the house?"
- "I heard Joseph isn't even working right now."
- "And that donkey. Huh, it's seen better days!"
- "Want to bet how long it will take to get your casserole dish back?"

How The Gospels Lied

All right, here's a quick exercise. Grab your copy of the Bible. If it's the New International Version, please flick through until you come to page 1110, the beginning of Gospel of Mark. Tell me, what does Mark write about the birth of Jesus? I'm waiting. Found it? You can't find anything can you? You mean to tell me that the first Gospel to write about the life of Jesus, the Gospel that Matthew and Luke copied from, makes absolutely no mention of the miraculous birth of Jesus Christ?

The first recorded biography of Jesus is completely and utterly silent on the birth of a human god? Well, that's what I thought you'd say. Now, if you're only gospel was Marks, which many early Christians only had, as he preceded the writings of the other Gospels by at least ten to twenty years, then you'd have no idea that Jesus was born of a virgin. You'd have no clue that his birth was anything but a standard mammal-esq conception and delivery or that he had a Midi-chlorian count in excess of 20,000, far higher than Master Yoda. Therefore, for at least forty years after the death of Jesus – not a single person had heard of the miraculous birth claim.

Now, I ask you this question: What credible biographer would examine all the facts of a man's biography and think to himself, "oh well, the part about him being born of a virgin is not significant"? It would be like an American

History writer including no mention of Native American Indians or the Battle of Little Bighorn in General Custer's biography. It simply wouldn't happen. So for 15 to 20 years after Jesus' death, no one on God's green earth had ever wrote anything that suggested that natural law was suspended to make way for the conception of Jesus. This prompted Thomas Paine to question humorously:

> *"Which do you believe more likely – that natural law was suspended (virgin birth) or that a Jewish minx lied?"*

Matthew and Luke are the only Gospels to make the virgin birth claim but they do so for different reasons, and in varying interpretations. Luke writes that Jesus is literally the Son of God. God impregnated Mary, so that her son was also God's son.

The narrative of Luke has the archangel Gabriel first delivering the news to John the Baptist's wife, Elisabeth, that she will soon bear child, despite the fact she believed herself to be barren, having tried unsuccessfully for child, for many years. In the sixth month of her pregnancy the angel then appears before Mary, "Greetings, you are highly favored! The Lord is with you", says Gabriel. This greeting troubled Mary, and the angel returned to comfort her:

> *"Do not be afraid, Mary, you have found favor with God. You will be with child and give birth to a son, and you are to give him the name Jesus. He will be great and will be called the Son of the Most High. The Lord God will give him the throne of his father David, and he will reign over the house of Jacob for ever; his kingdom will never end." (Luke 1:30-33 NIV)*

Mary then asks the angel quizzically, "How will this happen if I am a virgin?" The angel replied, "The Holy Spirit will come upon you, and the power of the Most High will over shadow you. So the Holy one to be born will be called the Son of God."

Hmm, was she consenting? It sounds like angel rape to me!

The above scripture is in stark contrast to Luke's fellow ideologue, Matthew, who gives his own interpretation on why Jesus was born of a virgin. Matthew, centrally concerned in appealing to a Jewish audience, is the only Gospel to go to extraordinary and nuanced lengths to match every story of Jesus' life to Old Testament prophecy. He believed that if he could show signs that Jesus was the fulfillment of Hebrew prophecy then the Jews would finally wake up and smell the metaphorical coffee.

Matthew's poor Hebrew linguistic skills (and we'll explore this again in later chapters), presumably because he was Greek, gets him caught up in some comical interpretative errors and rookie mistakes. So, why did Matthew write that Jesus was born to a virgin? It was because he found an obscure passage in the book of the prophet Isaiah that read:

"A virgin shall conceive and bear a son, and they shall call him Immanuel." (Isaiah 7:14 NIV)

This was Matthew's attempt at "Come all see what's written in the Hebrew Bible, and now look at the birth of Jesus. It must be true, he is the Messiah!" There are a couple of problems that Matthew runs right into. First and foremost, the passage from Isaiah was never intended to be a messianic prophecy; it was a prediction of an event that would occur in Isaiah's own lifetime. Isaiah wrote this passage to provide King Ahaz, who pre-dated Jesus by more than 800 years, encouragement that he would eventually be given victory over his enemies.

Isaiah documents that the House of David and King Ahaz were waging war against the Northern Kingdom of Israel, led by King Pegah, and the Kingdom of Israel led by King Retsin. The Bible records that Ahaz and Jerusalem were on the brink of defeat and facing destruction. God called for Isaiah to deliver a message to King Ahaz. The memo read, "I will send a deliverer to ensure the two hostile armies will fail in their attempt to capture the nation."

> *"Therefore the Lord himself will give you a sign: The virgin will be with child and will give birth to a son, and will call him Immanuel. He will eat curds and honey when he knows enough to reject the wrong and choose the right. But before the boy knows enough to reject the wrong and choose the right, the land of the two kings you dread will be laid waste." (Isaiah 7:14-16 NIV)*

Isaiah makes it crystal clear that the narrative was a prophecy about the failed siege of Jerusalem by the two attacking armies from the north. The last sentence, in particular, states that the two enemy nations will be defeated before the time that the child (Immanuel) will reach the age of maturity. Furthermore, two other Old Testament passages, namely 2 Kings 15:29-30, and 2 Kings 16:9, confirm that this prophecy was fulfilled with the assassination of the two respective kings. In other words, the fulfillment of this prophecy took place nearly eight centuries before the birth of Jesus, and had nothing to do with a future messianic prediction.

Henceforth, another piece in Matthew's puzzle to reverse engineer the story of Jesus to the Hebrew Bible.

Secondly, Matthew's Hebraic to Greek translation skills lets him down badly. The Hebrew word used in Isaiah is 'alma', meaning young woman. If read correctly, Isaiah was writing that a young woman shall conceive and bear a son. When Matthew interpreted 'alma' to mean virgin he subsequently used the Greek word for virgin, 'parthenos'. And this 2000-year myth was thus sealed with a typo.

The third major problem Matthew has, is when he quotes the verse from Isaiah into his birth of Jesus' narrative, going as far as to give the meaning to the name Immanuel – 'God's with us'. Immanuel Christ seems kind of odd, don't you think?

A question that has always bothered me, even beyond the points that I have raised thus far, is why does Jesus never make a single reference to his miraculous conception by his mother? As we will review in later chapters, Mary makes several appearances throughout the New Testament but never makes mention of her discussions with angels, or God, or her virginal conception. Furthermore, everything that Jesus ever says or does during his lifetime seems to come as complete surprise, if not shock, to her. Mary appears to have surprisingly low expectations of the son that she conceived in a game of midnight 'bury-the-bishop' with the Holy creator.

Unfortunately for the faithful, the discrepancies do not end here. In Luke's narrative, the angel Gabriel came to visit her to inform her that she'd soon be pregnant with God's child. The angel never says anything to Joseph; he is irrelevant in Luke's account. Whereas Matthew writes that Joseph became consumed with anger because his supposed virgin bride had informed him she was pregnant. Why not, it's only natural to presume wrongdoing in such a circumstance. But later that night as he considered his options, knowing that Mosaic law demanded he stone her to death on the city outskirts, an angel came to him:

> *"Joseph, son of David, do not be afraid to take Mary home as your wife, because what is conceived in her is from the Holy Spirit. She will give birth to a son and you shall name in Jesus, because he will save his people from their sins." (Matthew 1:20-21 NIV)*

This may seem like a petty observation on the surface but it illustrates the emergence of a pattern that features many irreconcilable discrepancies, and implausibility's. If we examine the actual birth (delivery) of Jesus, we read conflicting accounts that demonstrate that Matthew and Luke cannot both be right, given their respective conflicting narratives.

WISE MEN OR SHEPHERDS

Matthew says that the Wise Men (Magi) are led to Jerusalem by a star from the east. The star hovers above the city momentarily and the men ask some locals where the King of the Jews is to be born. King Herod learns of these star following strangers and enquires who they are and why are they looking for such a newborn. Matthew, reverting to his Hebrew Bible for a clue, gives the reason from prophecy, Micah 5:2:

> "But you, Bethlehem, in the land of Judah, are by no means least among the rulers of Judah; for out of you will come a ruler who will be the shepherd of my people Israel."

To take a side step from this narrative for a moment, the Gospels completely trip over themselves. Matthew in particular, attempts to place Jesus' birth in Bethlehem, the city of David, which again is nothing short of a vain plea to sway Jewish sensibilities. The fabrication of this story telling between Matthew and Luke is utterly soiled in John's Gospel, as he suggests that Jesus was neither born in Bethlehem nor descended from King David. As we can see once more, it is not possible for all Gospels to be right. At least one of them is telling a lie, but which one, and to what end?

This embellishment stems again from the fact that the Greek speaking Gospels failed to fully comprehend Hebrew, the language of the Old Testament (Torah in the Hebrew/Jewish tradition).

A Hebrew that should know is Hayyim ben Yehoshu, *'The Historical Basis of the Jesus Legend'* writes:

> "Since the early Christians believed that Jesus was the Messiah, they automatically believed that he was born in Bethlehem. But why did the Christians believe that he lived in Nazareth? The answer is quite simple. The early Greek speaking Christians did not know what the word "Nazarene" meant. The earliest Greek form of this word is

"Nazoraios," which is derived from "Natzoriya," the Aramaic equivalent of the Hebrew "Notzri." (Recall that "Yeishu ha-Notzri" is the original Hebrew for "Jesus the Nazarene.") The early Christians conjectured that "Nazarene" meant a person from Nazareth and so it was assumed that Jesus lived in Nazareth. Even today, Christians blithely confuse the Hebrew words "Notzri" (_Nazarene_, _Christian_), "Natzrati" _Nazarethite_) and "nazir" (_nazarite_), all of which have completely different meanings."

Anyway, the Star fires up its engines once again and points the men to the exact house in Nazareth... shit, Bethlehem where baby Jesus and his parents reside. A house is specified. In other words, there's no mention of a manger or stable. AN Wilson, in his book '*Jesus*' comments:

"The story of the baby being born in a stable at Bethlehem because there was no room for him at the inn is one of the most powerful myths ever given to the human race. A myth, however, is what it is. Even if we insist on taking every word of the Bible as literally true, we shall still not be able to find there the myth of Jesus being born in a stable. None of the Gospels state that he was born in a stable, and nearly all the details of the nativity scenes which have inspired great artists, and delighted generations of churchgoers on Christmas Eve, stem neither from history nor from Scripture, but from folklore. [...] Which is the more powerful figure of our imaginations - the 'real', historical Jesus of Nazareth, or the divine being, who in his great humility came down to be born as a poverty-stricken outcast?"

Now, have you ever thought how possible it was for a star to lead someone to an actual house? Considering that stars are hundreds, thousands, times larger than earth (notwithstanding that the nearest star – Alpha Centauri – is almost 17 freaking light-years away!), it's like giving directions of a new restaurant to a friend by saying, "It's located on the third rock from the sun. See you there at 7pm sharp."

Scholars believe the star mythology was borrowed from Zoroastrianism. This now mostly defunct religion was, until the rise of Islam, the national religion of the Iranian people (Persian) from the fourth to the sixth century. In Matthew's biblical narrative, the magi are given Zoroastrian titles and bear the same gifts as stated in Zoroastrian myth. Therefore, it seems likely that later scribes added this story into Matthew's Gospel, centuries after.

ANCIENT MYTHOLOGY

A study of ancient literature reveals that virgin birth mythologies were commonplace throughout the Arabian Peninsula and central Asia before, during, and after the commencement of the myth of Christianity. "The gods have lived on earth in the likeness of men" was a common saying among ancient pagans, a belief that supernatural events led to the existence of gods upon earth in human form.

The Egyptian god Horus was said to have been born to his virgin mother Isis. Attis, the Phrygian god, was said to be the son of the virgin Nana, who conceived him by putting in her bosom a ripe almond or pomegranate. Dionysus, the Grecian God, was said in one version of the myth concerning him to be the son of Zeus out of the virgin goddess Persephone. Jason, who was slain by Zeus, was said to have been another son of the virgin Persephone, and to have had no father, either human or divine. At the time when Christianity arose, all these gods were worshipped in various parts of the Roman Empire. It is well documented that religions with their origins in this part of the world borrowed mythology from one another. Christianity was not exempt from 'sharing' myth.

Don't forget that the likeness of God, the old dude with the flowing white hair and beard, is stolen from both Zeus (King of the Greek gods) and Jupiter (King of the Roman gods).

THE MURDER OF THE INNOCENTS

The wise men find the family in the house, offer their gifts and flee quickly to their home nations as an angel warned them in a dream that King Herod, fearful of a Jewish newborn king, would hunt them down and kill them. Matthew finds an obscure passage in the Old Testament to validate his story:

"Then was fulfilled that which was spoken through Jeremiah the prophet, saying, A voice was heard in Ramah, Weeping and great mourning, Rachel weeping for her children." (Matthew 2:18)

Similarly, Joseph receives the same dream; only the angel warns them that Herod has put out a decree that all Hebrew boys under the age of two are to be slaughtered. Joseph grabs his family and flees to Egypt for sanctuary, not to return until they learn of Herod's death some years later.

Where have you heard such a baby killing decree before? That's right, the story of Moses. The Pharaoh learns of a new born child that will one day become the Hebrew 'deliverer', and subsequently issues an edict that all Hebrew children under the age of two are to be executed. Moses' mother places him in a papyrus basket, and you know the rest of the story. This is Matthew at it again, trying to win his Jewish audience over with similarities to the most revered man in Jewish history, Moses. At the very least, you can't mock Matthew for trying.

Michael Grant, author of *Herod the Great* (1971), writes:

"The tale is not history but myth or folklore. Herod the Wicked, villain of many a legend, including the Massacre of the Innocents: the story is invented. Matthew's story of the Massacre of the Innocents by Herod the Great, because he was afraid of a child born in Bethlehem 'to be King of the Jews', is a myth allegedly fulfilling a prophecy by

Jeremiah and mirroring history's judgment of the great but evil potentate Herod."

Moreover, the story of a 'threatened child becomes a great leader' is commonplace amongst ancient literature and myth. It is the theme of Romulus & Remes, Sargon the Great, and Hercules, amongst many others. And now we see it reworked into the story of Jesus by one of his four nutty biographers.

Back to Luke again, and he says nothing of the family's exodus into Egypt. Moreover, his narrative is completely at odds with Matthews. Luke mentions nothing of wise men led by a star, but instead it's an unknown number of shepherds attending to their flocks in the fields that are descended upon by an angel. The angel says, "Today in the town of David a Savior has been born to you, he is Christ the Lord." The angel leads them to a manger, not a house, where baby Jesus is wrapped in blankets. Some more angels appear on the scene, they all give praise to baby Jesus, and that's the end of the scene. No star, no King Herod, no wise men, but plenty of angels.

At this same point in Luke's narrative, Matthew has the family fleeing into Egypt but Luke has 8-day-old Jesus presented at the Temple in Jerusalem to be circumcised. How can both accounts be right at this point? Who are we to believe?

Well, we can start by throwing out Matthew's account, as it is completely fallacious. Firstly, there are no ancient records or sources whatsoever that suggest that King Herod ever slaughtered children in or around Bethlehem, or anywhere else. In fact, historians such as Josephus, who maintained extensive records of Herod's numerous crimes, makes no mention of what would have unquestionably been his greatest atrocity, the murder of innocents. Does this mean Luke's account is more historically reliable? Well, not by any stretch! Luke's big mess up is his unique claim that there was an empire-wide census decreed by Caesar Augustus:

"In those days Caesar Augustus issued a decree that a census should be taken of the entire Roman world. This is the first census that took place while Quirinius was governor of Syria. And everyone went to his own town to register." (Luke 2:1-3 NIV)

Small problem, despite extensive records of Roman history, there is nothing to suggest that such a census ever took place. If it had, historians would know about it, but they don't. M Arnheim wrote in *Is Christianity True*:

"The Roman census would not have affected Nazareth in any case, as Galilee was not under Roman rule but had its own ruler, the 'tetrach' Herod Antipas, son of King Herod.'"

Can you imagine what such an event would have looked like? Millions of people across the entire European and African continents returning to their original towns of birth just to register that they're alive. Logistically improbable, most likely impossible! Certainly, the literary madness of writing about an event decades post the event, without the benefit of Wikipedia as a reference source, is self-evident.

Furthermore, Rome's purpose for any of the census' they conducted was to quantify the wealth of its citizenry so they could charge a tax. One's wealth is where is one resides, not where one's long lost ancestral home was. With this in mind, how could Rome possibly benefit by forcing tens of millions of people to travel to a place far from where their homes and businesses (i.e. their wealth) resided? It defies logic, and therefore it's just another sloppy error on behalf of sloppy Luke.

Luke was the only Biblical author who attempted to triangulate some kind of historicity, however. That said, he digs himself further into the historical dung heap with Luke

2:1-3 verse, insofar as his claim that Jesus' birth occurred during the time when Quirinius was governor of Syria. This is irreconcilable with Matthew's pronouncement - that it occurred during Herod's reign and makes the two gospels completely contradictory to one another.

We know for certain that Quirinius did not become governor of Syria until ten years after the death of Herod. Once again both Matthew and Luke cannot be correct. As close an admission as you will get from a devout Christian apologist, and distinguished biblical archaeologist G. Ernest Wright of Harvard Divinity School conceded: "This chronological problem has not been solved"

Talk about a reluctant willingness to surrender the point, but thankfully we do have an abundance of more open and forthright scholars such as Robin Lane Fox *The Unauthorized Version: Truth and Fiction in the Bible*:

"Quirinius, the governor of Syria whom Luke's Gospel mentions, is known from a careful history of affairs in Judea which was compiled by Josephus, an educated Jew, writing in Greek at Rome between c. 75 and c. 80. Josephus had his own prejudices and areas of interest, but he worked with a framework of hard facts which were freely available for checking and which he had collected responsibly. According to Josephus, Quirinius was governor of Syria with authority over Judea in AD 6, when the province was brought under direct Roman control. The year was a critical moment in Jewish history, as important to its province as the 1972 to Northern Ireland, the start of direct rule. On such a fact, at such a moment, Josephus and his sources cannot be brushed aside. There is however, an awkward problem. Luke's Gospel links Jesus' birth with Quirinius and with King Herod, but in AD 6 Herod had long disappeared. He had died soon after an eclipse of the moon, which is dated by astronomers to 12-13 March 4 BC, although a minority of scholars have argued for 5 BC instead. The

Gospel, therefore, assumes that Quirinius and King Herod were contemporaries, when they were separated by ten years or more."

GENEALOGY

A further conundrum, the respective authors Matthew and Luke find themselves in, is their attempts to include a genealogy for Jesus, whereas, Mark and John make no mention of his bloodline, and seemingly wisely. Why? Well, in short the genealogies of Matthew and Luke differ greatly. We will come to the contradictions shortly but for now let's highlight the most puzzling dilemma both have unwittingly created: if Jesus' mother conceived him as a virgin, as both writers claim she was, then this means, naturally, that Joseph wasn't Jesus' daddy. By direct implication this also means Jesus was not a blood-relative of Joseph.

But this fact doesn't stop Matthew and Luke from jumping under the bus, as both Gospels go forth and provide us with a genealogy of Jesus that does include Joseph's ancestry. If their stories were to maintain any credibility of consistency then his bloodline would travel only through Mary's ascendants. Matthew and Mark give no reason as to why they wrote what they wrote in regards to his bloodline, but what is of greater interest is their respective family trees provide conflicting records. Matthew has Jesus traced to his father Joseph, then to Joseph's father Jacob. Jesus' grandfather is Jacob right? Wrong, if you read Luke's account. Luke has Jesus' grandfather named as Heli.

Matthew: "and Jacob the father of Joseph, the husband of Mary, of whom was born Jesus, who is called Christ." (1:17)

Luke: "Jesus was the son, so it was thought, of Joseph, the son of Heli." (3:23)

The differences don't stop here. In Matthew, Jesus' great grandfather is Matthan, before him was Eleazar, onto Eliud, and on past. Whereas Luke says Jesus great grandfather is Mathat (possibly a scribe's typo), but then onto Levi then to Melchi. As you can see, this pair couldn't organize a cuddle in Amsterdam's red light district.

What I believe to be the real nail in the cross, as it were, is that Matthew traces Jesus' genealogy right back to King David and ultimately finishing with the founding patriarch of the Jewish religion (and effectively the monotheistic founder of Islam and Christianity), Abraham. Whereas Luke takes the family lineage all the way back to Adam, the first human to ever walk the planet. Even with the advent of modern day accounting I can only trace my forebears 150 years back, most probably because our family wanted to erase our bread thieving convict ancestry that had them involuntarily sent to Australia, but for Luke, without computer or DNA tracing technology, to go back 3,000 years is pretty darn impressive, if not outright ludicrous.

The comedy doesn't end there, however, if you go ahead and read the list of names included in Matthew's genealogy in Matthew 1:2-16, you'll find there are three sets of fourteen names. Matthew even makes a footnote to ensure the reader doesn't overlook this fact:

> *"Thus there were fourteen generations in all from Abraham to David, fourteen from David to the exile to Babylon, and fourteen from the exile to the Christ."*
> *(Matthew 1:17 NIV)*

At the risk of spelling it out to you, Abraham the father of Israel is born, fourteen generations later the most revered king of Israel, David, is born. Fourteen generations after David the collapse of the kingdom; and another fourteen generations after the exile we have, you guessed it, Jesus H Christ.

Ask yourself why the number fourteen, fourteen, fourteen? Well isn't it obvious? Matthew has carpentered Jesus' genealogy to demonstrate to his Jewish audience that something of great significance to the Hebrew people occurs every fourteen generations and after three such successions we have Jesus. Da-da!

Now we could leave this hack job here, as I think the point is pretty darn self-evident, but there's more fun to be had at Matthew's expense. If you now turn to page 1071 of your New International Version Bible, count the names in the third stanza of fourteen generations, from verses 1:2-16, you will find that there is only thirteen names. If Matthew's last name were Palin, I'm sure he too could see Russia from his backyard in Athens. What a pity too, he was doing so well...

The reader of the Bible must now ask himself the question; if the genealogies are meaningless then why did Matthew and Luke include them in their respective gospels? The simple answer, of course, is that the genealogies originally said that Jesus was the son of Joseph and thus Jesus fulfilled the messianic requirement of being a direct descendent of King David.

Considering we also know that the original manuscripts of the New Testament were tampered with, with bits added and deleted, it is evident that the founding Church lied. In the fourth century, the entire story of the virgin birth was fabricated and the church tried to cover it up with this patchwork of fictional lineage. Although, the virgin birth could be accommodated with the inclusion of a few added words into the genealogies to break the physical link between Joseph and Jesus, the Church was obviously cognizant of the fact that this would have simultaneously resulted in breaking the physical link between David and Jesus.

In leaving the genealogies as they are, however, the Church screwed itself by creating two irreconcilable problems:

1. Can you explain away the existence of two genealogies of Joseph, now rendered meaningless?
2. Can you explain how Jesus was a descendent of David if he was the product of a virgin birth?

We will review in later chapters that Paul, like John and Mark, was oblivious of the virgin birth and moreover, Paul wrote in his Romans epistle:

"Jesus was born of the seed of David." (Romans 1:3 NIV)

The word used in the Greek manuscript is "sperma". The same Greek word is translated in other verses as "offspring". This is the counter to some of the better-scripted argumentative Christians that will retort, "Oh but Joseph must have legally adopted Jesus". If this were the case Jesus would still not qualify as Messiah, as he had to be a physical descendent of King David through the male line. The 'sperma' was required according to biblical law.

Furthermore, don't be thinking that Jesus could be the "seed of David" through his mother Mary, as some apologists like to counter assert. This assertion violates the Hebrew law, as women did not count in reckoning descent for the simple reason that until the year 1827 AD it was believed, wrongly, that the complete human was present in the man's sperm. In other words, the female egg was unknown to mankind until the mid-nineteenth century. God flunked biology.

A clever analogy, I once heard, to explain the biblical view is that the woman's womb was the soil in which the seed was planted. Which is why women who were unable to fall pregnant in those times were labeled "barren", as in barren soil. It is also illustrated as such in the Book of Genesis:

"And I will put enmity between you and the woman, and between your seed and her seed." (3:15)

Which is why God executed Onan on the charge of murder, because Onan intentionally ejaculated all over the curtains and floor rugs rather than impregnate his sister-in-law:

"Then Judah said to Onan, "Lie with your brother's wife and fulfill your duty to her as a brother-in-law to produce offspring for your brother." But Onan knew that the offspring would not be his; so whenever he lay with his brother's wife, he spilled his semen on the ground to keep from producing offspring for his brother. What he did was wicked in the LORD's sight; so he put him to death also." (Genesis 38:8-10 NIV)

C'mon, I know we (man) didn't become aware of the fact that it required a woman's ovaries to form a human being, but you'd think God would've realized external ejaculation fell a few yards short of murder.

THE FOUR WOMEN

Ok, now it gets really interesting. We just covered that a woman's genealogy is not counted or considered under Hebrew Law, and we now know the reason why. But why then does Matthew include the names of four women in his genealogy of Jesus? I think I just heard you mutter "what the fuck?" under your breath. Because that's what I said when I discovered this. In Matthew's lineage of Jesus, are the women – Tamar, Rahab, Ruth, and Bathsheba. Who were these women?

Tamar: Performed an unconscionable sexual act that only a *Desperate Housewives* scriptwriter could have equaled. The Bible says her husband passed away, and she became desperate to preserve her husband's name. Her scheme? She pretended to be a prostitute, and lured her father-in-law into ravaging her. To whom she bore twins, one of whom was named Perez, who fits into the family line of Jesus. This tawdry event is amusingly spelt out in Genesis:

> *"When Judah saw her, he thought she was a prostitute, for she had covered her face. Not realizing that she was his daughter-in-law, he went over to her by the roadside and said, "Come now, let me sleep with you." "And what will you give me to sleep with you?" she asked. "I'll send you a young goat from my flock," he said. "Will you give me something as a pledge until you send it?" she asked. He said, "What pledge should I give you?" "Your seal and its cord, and the staff in your hand," she answered. So he gave them to her and slept with her, and she became pregnant by him." (Genesis 38:15-18 NIV)*

In other words, he shagged her for the price of one goat and his family tree. Oh, how sweet! Hang on; wouldn't this have invoked God's ire due to their blatant violation of one of his 613 commandments? Well, let us turn to the Book of Leviticus:

> *"If a man sleeps with his daughter-in-law, both of them must be put to death. What they have done is a perversion; their blood will be on their own heads." (Leviticus 20:12 NIV)*

Both of them are criminals in God's eyes, but they went unpunished. The end of this story, however, is she was successful, and if not for her devious actions the lineage to David then to Jesus would have apparently been affected.

Rahab: Fresh from ordering his army to perform a mass circumcision (imagine that discussion, Joshua, riding atop his horse, addresses his weary army, "Gents, we're almost ready to sack Jericho for our Lord, but I've had a revelation, I think God wants us to chop the top of our cocks off"… then a dude standing in the rear asks, "did he say we'd have to eat rocks?") Joshua was preparing to inflict his God inspired genocide on the residents of Jericho he sent in an advanced team of two spies. The two clandestine operatives stay the night inside Jericho's walls with Rahab the prostitute. She provides them "comfort", and a place of refuge as word had spread throughout the city that the Hebrews on the warpath.

> *"Then Joshua son of Nun secretly sent two spies from Shittim. "Go, look over the land," he said, "especially Jericho." So they went and entered the house of a prostitute named Rahab and stayed there." (Joshua 2:1 NIV)*

After the ancient Hebrews have completely and successfully ethnically cleansed' the entire city's occupants, Joshua provides Rahab and her family grace in return for her pre-genocide assistance.

Bathsheba: This is the woman most remembered for taking a bath, fully naked, atop her roof, in full view of King David's palace, in an effort to seduce the king to her lovely woman wobbly-bits. The king, like any other red-blooded Hebrew of the time, David had several hundred concubines for example, grabbed her and did the 'nasty thing', and her son carried on the family line to Jesus.

> *"One evening David got up from his bed and walked around on the roof of the palace. From the roof he saw a woman bathing. The woman was very beautiful, and David sent someone to find out about her. The man said, "Isn't this Bathsheba, the daughter of Eliam and the wife of Uriah the Hittite?" Then David sent messengers to get her. She came to him, and he slept with her. (She had purified herself from her uncleanness.) Then she went back home. The woman conceived and sent word to David, saying, "I am pregnant." (2 Samuel 11:2-5 NIV)*

Ruth: The only woman of the four without a tainted past, Ruth was a Moabite woman who married a Hebrew man, Boaz. It's a long story but the message is that Hebrew men could make a foreign woman turn good.

OF JOSEPH'S LOINS

Now, why would Matthew include four women, three guilty of some sort of sexual impropriety, and one a foreigner that the Hebrews detested? Why would Matthew mention these, and only these, women in his genealogy of Jesus? The only reason that makes any sense, **the only logical explanation is that Joseph impregnated Mary prior to them being married**. A fact evidently known to many at that time.

If people knew of Jesus' illegitimacy, it would have been used to counter the argument that he was the Messiah. By including these four "easy" women as ascendants of King David in Jesus' genealogy, the counter argument now becomes, "so what difference does one extra "easy" woman make in a bloodline full of them?

Even if we're wrong, and it seems highly improbable, at least we can lay claim Jesus came from a long line of sexual deviates! Nice.

CIRCUMCISION OF JESUS

Insofar as the circumcision of Jesus is concerned, this is a story that is completely exclusive to Luke. The other Gospels make no mention, not even the plagiarizer Matthew. The narrative has the eight days old Jesus presented at the Temple to a priest by the name of Simeon. Luke alleges that God had promised Simeon that he would not die until he had circumcised the new king of Israel, that being Jesus. Receiving baby Jesus with both arms, the priest gave the following rendition:

> *"Sovereign Lord, as you have promised, you now dismiss your servant in peace. For my eyes have seen your salvation, which you have prepared in the sight of all people, a light for revelation to the Gentiles and for glory to your people Israel." (Luke 2:29-32 NIV)*

The passage below this reads:

"The child's father and mother marveled at what was said about him." (Luke 2:30 NIV)

Again Luke covertly slips in referring to Joseph as Jesus' father, again, but more significantly, how is it that the above words of the priest would've caused Mary to marvel? This is a woman that according to Luke, had been previously foretold by an angel she would conceive God's son without the necessity of sweaty non-air-conditioned Palestinian sex with a short, fat, hairy and sweaty Palestinian man. Then on the day of Jesus' birth, her son's arrival is celebrated by umpteen numbers of angels and mystery shepherds led by spirits. But now all of a sudden, she is said to be amazed at a mere few words given by a priest? It really just seems completely arbitrary, doesn't it?

Ultimately, we have demonstrated in just the opening stanza of Jesus' recorded life that his biographers were merely human, and were not exempt from making super-human errors. Any Christian that continues to maintain the position that the Bible is the inerrant word of God, past this point, has had their argument ravaged by the very authors who wrote the thing. A single error, discrepancy, contradiction or incorrect historical claim eliminates the Bible's claim of inerrancy, and we have already illustrated this most beautifully. But stay tuned, as there is more fun to come!

Time for Another Joke

A woman takes her 16-year-old daughter to the doctor. The doctor says, "Okay, Mrs. Jones, what's the problem?"

The mother says, "It's my daughter; Darla. She keeps getting these... cravings, she's putting on weight and is sick most mornings."

The doctor gives Darla a good examination then turns to the mother and says, "Well, I don't know how to tell you this but your Darla is pregnant. About 4 months would be my guess."

The mother says, "Pregnant? She can't be, she has never ever been left alone with a man! Have you Darla?"

Darla says, "No mother! I've never even kissed a man!"

The doctor walked over to the window and just stares out it. About five minutes pass and finally the mother says, "Is there something wrong out there doctor?"

The doctor replies, "No, not really, it's just that the last time anything like this happened, a star appeared in the east and three wise men came over the hill. I'll be damned if I'm going to miss it this time!"

CHAPTER FIVE

The Gospels on Jesus' Adolescent Years

What Christians Know

What do Christians know about the young boy, Jesus? Not much, as there is little to know of Jesus' adolescent years using only the New Testament as your reference. If we exclude the one narrative mentioned in Luke, these years, Jesus aged 13-30, are indeed his 'missing years'.

The Joke

Jesus travels to India during his missing formative years. He meets with Krishna and an old white bearded man. It's a Saturday so they decide to play a round of golf at the Mumbai Country Club. All three players are approximately 180 yards short of the green on the longest par 5 of the course. Krishna turns to Jesus, and the bearded dude, "Lads, $100 to whoever can hit nearest the pin from here."

The bet is locked in. Krishna pulls out his 6 iron and shanks his shot into the water guarding the front side of the green. Unperturbed, he walks to the edge of the water, closes his eyes, then levitates himself across the water, pulls out a pitching wedge, and hits the ball onto the green, 6 feet from the flag, all without getting a single drop of water on himself.

Jesus is up next. Like Krishna his approach falls into the water. Jesus unconcerned, walks to the edge of the pond, steps across the surface of the water, pulls out his wedge, and presto he is now 4 feet from the hole.

Finally, the old bearded guy plays his. The ball sails towards the water, as it is about to make its entry into the pond, a frog jumps up and grabs the ball in its mouth. Watching on was an opportunistic eagle, who swooped on the frog taking him his mouth. The eagle swallowed the frog, then flew above the green and pooped out the ball before landing in the centre of the hole with a 'plop'.

Krishna turned to Jesus, and said, "This is the last time I ever play with your Dad!"

How The Gospels Lied

Without doubt, this should be the shortest chapter in this book as Luke is the only Gospel to make any mention of Jesus between his ages two to thirty-three. I find the following to be a mind shattering observation; God, according to Christian belief, gave birth to a human son, and not a single writer of that period, of which there were hundreds of historians floating about Jerusalem at that time, thought it relevant to write about his childhood, his teenage years, or most of his adulthood. Thus we have no bloody idea what trials or tribulations or dead hookers and uncut Columbian cocaine Jesus went through to become the arrogant self-righteous preacher we all know and love.

Was he a pimply awkward adolescent that refused to do his chores? Was he bad at sports? Did chicks dig him? Did he play 'spin-the-bottle' with the other teenagers in his village? Did he experiment with mushrooms and peyote? We know none of any of this and the only story we do have of the missing years [from the bible, there is some text in the Gnostic texts and in the Infancy Gospels of Thomas] of Jesus is the one Luke tells of Jesus as a twelve year old. Luke writes that every year Joseph and Mary would travel from Nazareth to Jerusalem for the Feast of the Passover. This is a pretty normal family outing for a Jewish holiday it would seem, but this story takes a fast turn for nonsense when he writes:

"After the Feast was over, while his parents were returning home, the boy Jesus stayed behind in Jerusalem, but his parents were unaware of it. Thinking he was in their company, they traveled on for a day. Then they began looking for him among their friends and relatives. When they did not find him they returned to Jerusalem to look for him there." (Luke 2:43-44 NIV)

How drunk or stoned would Joseph and Mary have had to have been to mistakenly believe that Jesus was right there with them (or perhaps he was there in spirit), when he clearly wasn't? And if they weren't at all intoxicated, as would have been the custom whilst 'on the road', then did they just simply not give a shit? Naturally, you would presume that if Mary believed herself to be raising God's little Buddha, she'd be an extremely over-protective parent. My parents were over-protective raising me, for example, and I can assure you that they did not believe me to be a saint or much less godly. Thankfully, there was no Department of Child Welfare back then, or this set of parents would be without a child.

The story continues that his irresponsible guardians return to Jerusalem to find him. At the end of the third day of looking for him (Mary searched the markets and Temples. Joseph thought it would be best if he checked the whore houses...alone), they found the adolescent Jesus preaching to several gathered Jews at the Temple.

The young Jesus' wisdom astonished those who listened, and the priests were said to have been amazed that a youth would have such insight and wisdom. Again, if this guy was at all a child prodigy then why didn't anyone take down any notes? For later reference, the fact that Luke writes Jesus was found on the third day is no accident.

Joseph and Mary, upon finding him at the Temple, yell to him (as all parents do when their kid disappears):

*"Son, why have you treated us like this? Your father and I
have been anxiously searching for you." (Luke 2:48 NIV)*

If Jesus had any spunk at all, his reply should have been,
"Where was I? I am only twelve years of age, you are my
goddamn father and it was you that bloody well left me
here, father of the fucking year!"

It's interesting that Luke writes that "his father",
Joseph, had been looking for him? Why would Luke write
that if he meant what he said, earlier in his Gospel, that
Jesus was the Son of God? Is this a telling slip of the pen or
concentration as he copied other sections of Mark's Gospel
that refers to Jesus as the son of Joseph? Nevertheless,
Jesus replies to his now concerned parents, who didn't
seem all that concerned for his absence for at least the day
or two when they thought he was still in the backseat of
the car playing with his Gameboy™ (which is the ancient
Hebrew term for 'penis'):

*"Why were you searching for me? Didn't you know I had
to be in my Father's house?" (Luke 2:49 NIV)*

The punch line of Luke's story is one that always elicits a
quiet giggle from me:

*"But they (Joseph and Mary) did not understand what he
was saying to them." (Luke 2:50 NIV)*

Which means, all sarcasm aside, that his parents believed
he was a babbling lunatic... he was probably speaking in
tongues, Evangelical Christian style!

Anyway, that's all we have on Jesus as a child. Not a
single narrative of the mystical man from this age until he
abruptly reenters the scene in his early 30's. Eighteen years
of complete silence. His formative years are unknown. Did
people stop paying attention to him? Was he unworthy of
notoriety as a teenager? Had he not yet harnessed his
magical powers, leading him in need of rescue from the
Dead Sea lifeguards whenever he attempted to make an
aqua crossing

Some eccentrics hold the view that Jesus spent his 'missing years' wandering throughout India and Tibet learning their form of mysticism and primitive medicine. Obviously, this is nothing more than conjecture as there is absolutely no evidence to substantiate such a claim. A Christian Evangelical group even swayed Universal Studios to part with some cold hard cash to film a documentary in search of Jesus' footsteps in Tibet, but they came back with nothing to show for their determined (misguided) efforts.

Another more fanciful theory claims Jesus visited the UK, then known as Albion or Britannia, with his father Joseph. Legend has it that together they sailed up what is now Glastonbury in the south west of the England. Whilst again, there is absolutely zero evidence to support such a trip took place, it does get some Christian happy clappers excited because there are some historical possibilities (*cough* bullshit) to hang their hat on. That being that there was a significant amount of trade done between Britannia and Judea as both were colonies of the Roman Empire, but that's about the extent to the historical plausibility. Hardly a smoking gun, but probably enough for a Dan Brown enthusiast to get all hot and bothered… yeah, I went there!

GOSPEL OF THOMAS

The Gospel According to Thomas, commonly shortened to the *Gospel of Thomas*, is a well-preserved manuscript discovered near Nag Hammadi, Egypt, in December 1945, in one of a group of books known as the Nag Hammadi library. This library contained hundreds of copies of the Hebraic Old Testament (Torah) and many other significant records from the ancient tribes.

The Gospel of Thomas is very different in tone and structure from the four Canonical Gospels. Unlike the canonical Gospels, it is not a narrative account of the life of

Jesus; instead, it consists of sayings attributed to Jesus, sometimes stand-alone, sometimes embedded in short dialogues or parables.

This gospel was one of those omitted by the Council of Nicea in AD 322, and you will soon discover why. The writings of Thomas provide us with a description of Jesus aged five to seven years of age. Reading this gospel conjures images from Monty Python's Life of Brian, "He's not the messiah, he's just a very naughty boy!" Thomas certainly leaves us with such an impression.

There is a bunch of narratives that present the Child Messiah as a mischievous, petulant, disobedient little shit who used his magical powers to circumvent natural laws ad hoc, and for his own personal gain. We will never know for certain the reasons why the Nicea Council elected to omit this gospel, as it would have complimented Matthew, Mark, Luke, and John's respective lack of childhood biography, but we can presume it because Thomas is forthright in asserting that Joseph was the father of Jesus.

The opening of Thomas begins:

"I, Thomas the Israelite, tell unto you, even all the brethren that are of the Gentiles (Non-Jews), to make known unto you the works of the childhood of our Lord Jesus Christ and his mighty deeds, even all that he did when he was born in our land: whereof the beginning is thus:"

Chapters 1-2: Thomas' opening story is of Jesus aged five. We read the toddler playing on the banks of a small stream, using his apparent wizardry; he diverted the running water into a number of different pools using his mind. Oooh, amazing! But this is just an entrée of more delicious things to come. Next thing, an old man notices the toddler in the shallows "playing upon the Sabbath", and runs to report Jesus' illegal activity to his father:

*"Joseph, lo, thy child is at the brook, and he hath taken
clay and fashioned twelve little birds, and hath polluted
the Sabbath day."*

Joseph, alarmed, runs to where his son is playing and
cried, *"Wherefore doest thou these things on the Sabbath, which
it is not lawful to do?"* His five-year-old son does not utter a
single word in reply to Joseph, and instead clapped his
hands together and cried out to the clay model sparrows to
become alive. And alive they became, before singing a
song and then taking flight. Joseph and the old man were
amazed, and ran to the town's chief to inform what this
young prodigy had just accomplished.

Wow! Let's take a moment to think about this. Jesus
brought to life birds made from mud. Now, where have I
heard this before? Let me think…

*"Now the Lord God had formed out of the ground all the
beasts of the land and all the birds of the air." (Genesis
2:19 NIV)*

That's right, God made the birds from clay on day 5 of
creating the universe. It appears Thomas could read, as he
had read the Old Testament well.

Chapter 3: Not everyone was impressed by the young
lad's mystical achievement. In fact, the son of Annas The
Scribe took particular umbrage to the young Jewish boy
who would dare to play games on the Lord's Day. Annas
Jr. jumped down into the muddy pools, and dispersed the
water, which Jesus had gathered together. Most five year
olds would be glad for this lenient punishment
considering a stoning was warranted under Mosaic Law,
but little Jesus couldn't keep his mouth shut, and replied
angrily:

*"O evil, ungodly, and foolish one, what hurt did the pools
and the waters do thee?"*

Now, that certainly warrants a stoning. Moses would be so pissed right now! But Jesus doesn't stop there. He casts a spell on the man's son:

"Behold, now also thou shalt be withered like a tree, and shalt bear leaves, neither root, nor fruit."

Immediately the young boy began to whither up into an old man before their very eyes. Annas Junior, fell the ground and wailed, *"How could a child do such a terrible deed?"*... well duh, Annas, what else is the son of a genocidal, infanticidal, megalomaniacal, malevolent dictator who wants to see all non-Jews burn in hell for all eternity going to do? Call a tickle fight?

Chapter 4: Shortly after turning a fellow young man from his village into an old man, Jesus was running through the streets of his village, when a random child accidently ran into Jesus, bumping his shoulder. Jesus turned towards the unobservant youth and shouted:

"Thou shalt not live a full life!"

With that curse, the young boy fell to the ground and died.

Jesus has now murdered two children by age 5, just in case you wanted to keep a body count. Aww, he's so cute, growing up to be just like his sky-daddy! The bereaved parents of the deceased arrived on Joseph's doorstep, with their dead son in their arms, and cried, *"Your son can no longer live in this village if you can't teach him how to bless rather than curse, for he is killing kids."*

Chapter 5: Joseph was irate with his murderous son, grabbing the young Jesus by the ear, and shouted, *"Who does such a terrible thing, that would bring hate upon this family?"* Jesus replied, somewhat sheepishly, *"I know you don't understand, but nevertheless for the sake of keeping the peace I will refrain from similar actions in the future. But just know that those two kids had it coming to them."*

The irate Joseph grabbed his son and threw him aside, to which Jesus responded venomously, *"Your actions towards me are unwise. You don't know who I am."* To which Joseph replies, *"but I know who you are, you're a little thug. Is what you are, buddy?"*

Chapter 6: A teacher by the name Zacchaeus, marveled at how the boy Jesus spoke to his father. Not marvel as in 'your son needs a spanking' kind of way, but more in a 'your son is so wise for his age' kind of way. These people had to have been fricking high!

This Zaccaeus fellow asks Joseph if he may teach his son the alphabet, *"Your son is very wise, and he has great understanding. I will teach him all the letters and impart further knowledge upon him."*

The teacher began with the letter A (alpha), and that's as far as the first lesson got, before Jesus shouted at Zacchaeus, *"Why are you going to teach me the letter B (beta), next, when you don't even understand what A means. You are a stupid hypocrite."* There's no letting up with this kid! The teacher was amazed and horrified at the same time.

Chapter 7: Zacchaeus returned the petulant and obnoxious child to his father Joseph with a note that read, *"Take him away my brother Joseph. I cannot endure the severity of his look. He ridicules everything that I have to say. This young child is not of this earth. I cannot follow his understanding. He is either a god or an angel, I cannot determine, but he has made me look foolish."*

Chapter 8: Zacchaeus, now a broken man, sought the consul of his village peers, but the young Jesus pursued his former teacher mocking and taunting him wherever he went. *"Now let us see who really are the foolish and the wise. I am above you, and if I want to curse you then I will. No one shall stop me."*

Chapter 9: A few days later, Jesus was playing with some other youngsters in the upper story of someone's house, when suddenly one of the kiddies falls from the top tier to his death. Oh boy, he's done it again! All the other children fled the scene when they had seen what happened, and Jesus waited at the house, alone under his bed, until the parents of the deceased child returned home.

The parents accused Jesus of murdering their only son, to which he replied, *"I did not push him!"* But they did not believe him. Jesus then leaped from the roof to where the boy's body laid on the ground. Jesus yelled out, *"Zeno (the boy's name), arise from the dead, and tell me, did I push you to your death?"* The boy miraculously came to life and replied, *"No, you did not push me down, but you raised me up."* Thomas then adds that the boy's family gave worship to God, and from that day began to praise the young Jesus.

In the event you are keeping score; two killed, one saved.

That said, this raises an interesting character flaw in young Jesus. While he was clearly completely able to circumvent the laws of nature and resurrect this poor lad, apparently one of Jesus' friends, post being splattered on the ground, he didn't. It wasn't until his character was questioned that he decided to 'raise him up'. Suggesting that God does possess the power to circumvent natural disasters, Hitler, pedophile priests, but doesn't... not even when his character is questioned.

Chapter 10: A few days later a young man of the village was chopping wood when the axe caught the instep of his foot, causing blood to shoot out profusely. The five-year-old Jesus pushed his way past the crowd to assist the bleeding man. As soon as Jesus' laid hands on the man, the bleeding ceased. Jesus turned on his heels and gave the parting words, *"Continue chopping the wood but remember me."* So much for humility, huh? Actually, I wonder if 'chopping the wood' was a euphemism for 'whacking-off' and that's why Jesus, the only gay in the village, wanted the man 'chopping his wood' to remember him. These are serious questions.

JESUS LIED – HE WAS ONLY HUMAN

Chapter 11: Jesus is now six years of age and is carrying two gourds of water for his mother. I use the term 'mother' because Thomas doesn't even mention her by name. So much for the great lady of the Catholic Church! Anyway, Jesus trips, causing a crack in one of the gourds. Jesus took off his shirt, laid it upon the ground, and poured the contents of water into his shirt before bringing the contents to his mother. Which is Mary, in case you forgot.

Thomas then writes:

"His mother saw what was done, she kissed him; and she kept with herself the mysteries which she saw him do."

Chapter 12: Thomas writes a story of a now eight-year-old Jesus that is sowing wheat with his father in the fields. Jesus magically turns one lot of wheat into a hundred measures. With his miraculously produced surplus food, Joseph invites all the poor people of the village to his house so that they may eat. This is obviously a story that echoes the later alleged miracles whereby Jesus feeds the masses with a single loaf of bread and one or two baitfish.

Chapter 13: Joseph was asked by a rich man of the village to make him a yoke from two beams of wood. Joseph accidentally cut one piece too short to accomplish the task ("measure twice, cut once, dumb-ass") and in his frustration goes to find his son. Jesus says, *"Father, let me see if I can figure this out."* Jesus placed his hands on the wood, and the timber magically grew the required length, right there before Joseph's eyes. Joseph was stunned, embraced his son, and proclaimed, *"Happy I am that God has given me my son."*

Later that evening, after Joseph tells his wife about Jesus' magical wood lengthening skills, Mary asks her son, on behalf of her all-women's knitting club, if he is able to provide the same wood lengthening trick on Hebrew men. Not really.

Nonetheless, I am not sure why this wood magic feat would have come as a big surprise given that his father had seem him fashion birds out of mud, earlier.

Chapter 14: Joseph, although happy with his son's phenomenal magical powers, was becoming distressed that Jesus had still not learnt how to read or write. So, he sent him to another teacher to learn the Hebrew and Greek alphabets. Similar to the story of the hapless teacher Zaccaheus, Jesus said to his new teacher, *"If you know the alphabet so well, tell me the power of Alpha, and I will tell you the power of Beta."*

The teacher became furious at such insubordination from his trying pupil, and smacked him atop the head with a stick. Jesus rubbed his head in pain, and then cursed him out of vengeance, killing the teacher on the spot with laser bolts from his eyes, like Superman. That's now three confirmed kills, and is yet to hit his difficult teen years. Brace. Brace. Brace!

Chapter 15: With one teacher institutionalized, and another dead at the hands of the mischievous young Jesus, it is surprising that a third stepped forward to offer educational guidance for the young prodigy, struggling with his wizardry. Joseph offered a word of warning, however, *"If you have no fear of him, then please take him and teach him."* On his first day in class and without having learnt more than two letters of the alphabet, Jesus picked up a book of the law, and read the entire Law of Deuteronomy to the class. The classroom was amazed, and *"marveled at the beauty of his teaching and the readiness of his words"*, considering the fact he was so young and uneducated. Knowing his son's violent history, Joseph became afraid, fearing this new teacher to be headed to a similar fate of his two predecessors. Joseph went to the class to take his child home. But the teacher said, *"Your son is full of grace and wisdom."* By wisdom I assume he means sociopathic behavior.

Chapter 16: This is certainly the most revealing chapter of all, in my opinion, outside of the canonized gospels of the New Testament. It not only illustrates a narrative between Jesus and his brother, James, but it suggests that James is the elder of the two. I am sure you see where I am going with this? If James is the elder then how on earth could his mother Mary have been a virgin when she conceived Jesus?

While the passage in question doesn't say outright that James is the elder, it follows reasonable logic when you read:

> *"And Joseph sent his son James to bind fuel and carry it into his house. And the young child Jesus also followed him."*

This is an instruction from father to one son, with the other son following his big strong brother. The reversing of this sentence would hardly make logical sense would it? Would Joseph give orders to the youngest, for a physical task, and the elder followed the younger? No, why would you even suggest that? *High fives all round*.

The story continues with James being bitten on the hand by a snake, Jesus rushes to his aid just in time to save his elder brother's life. He breathes on the wound and James is immediately healed and the snake's head spontaneously combusts and Mary gets a nice new pair of snake-leather shoes.

Chapter 17: Here we learn of Jesus' second resurrection miracle, as he brings back from the dead a child that had fallen sick and perished. Jesus grabbed the dead boy's hand, and said, *"I say unto thee, Child, die not, but live and be with your mother."* Immediately, the boy sat up, laughed and hugged his mother. All the onlookers marveled, and said, *"This young child is either a god or an angel of God."* Jesus walked off as if what he had just done was no big deal to go play with some nearby children and push them off the rooftops.

Chapter 18: Jesus starts to get the hang of the raising people from the dead business, as it was only a short time later Jesus walked past a work site to find a man lying dead on the ground. Jesus picked up his hand, *"Arise and get back to work!"* The other workers watching on were naturally astonished, and said, *"This young child is from heaven."* Naturally! Well, why wouldn't he be? Duh!

Chapter 19: Thomas corroborates Luke's account of Jesus being left at the Temple in Jerusalem during the Festival of the Passover.

So, there you have the Gospel of Thomas, filled with stories of Jesus' impetuous and bi-polar nature. It really annoys me this book wasn't adopted by the Council of Nicea as it portrays Jesus as a bad-ass mofo who doesn't take shit from anyone. This would have only broadened his appeal to weekend rugby players.

CHAPTER SIX

The Gospels on Jesus' Baptism

What Christians Know

John the Baptist baptized Jesus in the River Jordan to mark the beginning of his ministry.

The Joke

A burglar sneaks in a dark bar (after hours) and goes right for the cash register.

A voice calls out, "GOD IS WATCHING YOU".

He looks all around and sees nothing so returns to jimmying the cash drawer. Again, the voice says, "GOD IS WATCHING YOU".

The burglar looks around and finally sees a parrot in a cage and says, "Oh, Hi Polly. You startled me."

"Hey" said the parrot. "My name ain't Polly. It's John the Baptist."

The burglar snorted, "Who in the world named you John the Baptist?"

Parrot says, "The same guy who named that Rottweiler over there, GOD!"

How The Gospels Lied

John the Baptist was a fire and brimstone preacher that led a movement of Baptism at the Jordan River in expectation of an 'end of days' divine apocalypse. He foretold the arrival of a messiah who would end the Roman occupation of Israel.

He was obviously a big fan of the Old Testament prophets as he very much mimicked their eccentric methods for promoting prophecy and challenging sinful rulers. Mind you, he wasn't as cool as the Prophet Ezekiel, who ate shit sandwiches for two years to return the Jews to God's service. Nonetheless, Mark's Gospel describes him thus:

"John wore clothing made of camel's hair, with a leather belt around his waist, and he ate locusts and wild honey." (Mark 1:6 NIV).

Luke is the first to introduce us to John the Baptist, in his narrative of Mary's conception. He begins his Gospel by describing an elderly childless couple, the priest Zechariah and his wife Elizabeth. As Zechariah is on his knees giving praise to the Almighty in the Temple, he sees the angel Gabriel, who tells him that he and his wife will have a son who will be a great prophet, and will go before the Lord "like Elijah."

Zechariah returned home to discover his wife had conceived a child. A miracle! Approximately six months later, Gabriel appeared to the Virgin Mary, the cousin of Elizabeth, and told her that she was about to bear a son who would be called "Son of the Most High, a king whose kingdom would never end." Thus Elizabeth gave birth to John, and Mary gave birth six months later to Jesus. Thus, the two wunderkinds were cousins.

After describing the birth of John, Luke says that Jesus grew and "was in the wilderness until the day of his showing to Israel."

Central to John the Baptist's teaching, was the doctrine that one must repent for their sins and beg for forgiveness. The dunking of one in the water was symbolic atonement. This was his baby, he owned this ritual. John the Baptist was Jesus' New Testament apocalyptic prophet predecessor, as he too promised the world was coming to an end, saying; *"Repent for the kingdom of heaven is near"*.

It is he that introduces us the concept of Hell, and the doctrine of eternal torture to Christianity:

"But when he saw many of the Pharisees and Sadducees coming to where he was baptizing, he said to them: "You brood of vipers! Who warned you to flee from the coming wrath? Produce fruit in keeping with repentance. And do not think you can say to yourselves, 'We have Abraham as our father.' I tell you that out of these stones God can raise up children for Abraham. The ax is already at the root of the trees, and every tree that does not produce good fruit will be cut down and thrown into the fire.

I baptize you with water for repentance. But after me will come one who is more powerful than I, whose sandals I am not fit to carry. He will baptize you with the Holy Spirit and with fire. His winnowing fork is in his hand, and he will clear his threshing floor, gathering his wheat into the barn and burning up the chaff with unquenchable fire."
(Matthew 3:7-12 NIV)

Got to love those words; "unquenchable fire", the promise of infinite suffering, right? This becomes a major tenet of Jesus' teaching thus we will cover more on this heinous, and morally depraved fear mongering in later chapters.

The Synoptic Gospels write that John the Baptist was forewarned by the prophecy of Isaiah (40:3) that Jesus will one day make way for him:

"A voice of one calling in the desert, prepare the way for the Lord, make straight paths for him."

I hope by now you can see how easy it is to write a biography about someone a hundred years post his or her death. You can even use passages from a book, such as the Hebrew Bible, to harmonize the story to ensure certain events come out right. The prophecy of Isaiah, as the Gospels disingenuously use it, reminds me an old joke:

A man who thought he was John the Baptist was disturbing the neighborhood, so for public safety, he was committed. He was put in a room with another crazy and immediately began his routine, "I am John the Baptist!

Jesus Christ has sent me!" The other guy looks at him and declares, "I did not!"

Mark, writing before the other Gospels, creates a theological pothole for the early Christians, as he writes:

"And so John came, baptizing in the desert region and preaching baptism of repentance for the forgiveness of sins." (Mark 1:4 NIV)

What, the repentance of sins? Then why does Jesus need to be baptized if he was "born without sin"? Oh Mark, you dropped the ball there, buddy. Thankfully, Matthew spots this conundrum when writing his account, and adds a few sentences in an effort to sweep Mark's error under the carpet. Instead, his narrative has John the Baptist protesting that it is he that should be baptized by Jesus, and not the other way round:

"But John tried to deter him, saying, "I need to be baptized by you, and do you come to me?" Jesus replied, "Let it be so now; it is proper for us to do this to fulfill all righteousness." Then John consented."
(Matthew 3:14-15 NIV)

Thanks to Matthew's observation and correction of Mark's passage, Christians can breathe a moment's sigh of relief, for now.

The baptism is the first event of Jesus' biography whereby all four Gospels give an account. However, the baptism itself is only mentioned in passing rather than narrated by the Gospel John.

The other three Gospels give similar narratives of the baptism, for the most part, including the opening of the heavens upon Jesus' emerging from the water. Then there is the appearance of a dove, before a voice from the sky begins to speak. It's here, however, that the three amigos take divergent paths. As Jesus emerges from the water held in the arms of John the Baptist, what does God say from Heaven?

Matthew: "And a voice from heaven said, "This is my Son, whom I love; with him I am well pleased." (3:17)

Mark: "And there came a voice from heaven, saying, "You are my Son, in whom I am well pleased." (1:11)

Luke: "And there a voice came from heaven saying, "You are my Son, today I have begotten you." (3:22)

Given a quick glance, each of the Gospels accounts do indeed sound similar, if not somewhat identical. I can assure you, however, that these lone few verses contain some very deceptive theological discrepancies. In Matthew, it is as if God is speaking to John the Baptist directly, giving him and the curious onlookers along the shore confirmation that this is the Messiah. In other words, God is not speaking directly to Jesus.

Whereas Mark and Luke have God is speaking directly to Jesus, thereby confirming his identity as the son of Sky-Pixie. This seems reasonable enough, if, for example, your friends and family were hell bent on convincing you that you were the Son of God, you'd probably want confirmation from the celestial father figure that you weren't merely over self-medicating on the Zoloft™.

This being a further illustration that not all Gospels can be correct; at absolute least, one must be wrong. A further problem I have with this baptism narrative, at least from a historical perspective, is that Mark writes that enormous crowds would flock, everyday, to watch John the Baptist perform his dunking water show, as the people were amazed with his preaching's of repentance and forgiveness:

"The whole Judean countryside all the people of Jerusalem went out to him" (Mark 1:5 NIV)

Matthew and Luke make similar statements but none include a passage in regards to the day Jesus was baptized, "On this day the crowds were gone. Jesus' baptism was done in strict privacy". In strict privacy? How is this possible? Because neither John the Baptist nor Jesus write about their meeting. Therefore there had to have been witnesses. But if there were onlookers, how come no one bothered to write about what he or she witnessed?

Surely someone couldn't have waited to get home to write in his or her journal the following entry:

"Dear Diary, holy shit you are not going to believe this, but today a guy named Jesus was baptized in the Jordan, and as he emerged from the water God spoke and we all heard it. He has a surprisingly nasally voice and I couldn't determine from where his accent came, but I heard him. What a day. Time for bed, I am pooped."

John continued to preach - calling on everyone to repent - that is until his arrest by King Herod. Whilst in prison, John sent his followers to ask Jesus, *"Are you he that is to come, or is there another?"*

Effectively, John was asking:

"It was revealed to me in a vision that you are the promised deliverer, but I expected or hoped you would have punted Herod and the Romans by now, thus commencing the reconstruction of the kingdom of David. But here I sit in a dirty, damp cell, with no deliverance in sight. Is there someone else to come after you? Are you just the entrée to the main course? I await your response. Help me Obe Wan Kinobe-Jesus, you're my only hope…"

Jesus gave the following reply:

"Go back and report to John what you hear and see: The blind receive sight, the lame walk, those who have leprosy are cured, the deaf hear, the dead are raised, and the good news is preached to the poor." (Matthew 11:5 NIV)

This was Jesus' way of communicating to John the Baptist that he indeed saw himself as the promised Messiah. And that he truly believed John's prophesized end of day's apocalypse was within sight.

Before we progress too far, let us make a quick backtrack to examine the contradicting accounts of the Gospels as they independently retell what events transpired *the day after* John had baptized Jesus in the Jordan River.

What Happens the Day After?

The plot twists again, this time in relation to the events that transpire the day after Jesus' baptism. The Synoptic Gospels, Matthew, Mark, and Luke, all pretty much say the same thing:

> *Mark: "At once the Spirit sent him out into the desert, and he was in the desert forty days, being tempted by Satan. He was with the wild animals, and angels attended him." (1:12-13)*

> *Matthew: "Then Jesus was led by the Spirit into the desert to be tempted by the devil." (4:1)*

> *Luke: "Jesus, full of the Holy Spirit, returned from the Jordan and was led by the Spirit in the desert, where for forty days he was tempted by the devil." (4:1)*

Ok, the trio maintains some consistency on what takes place the day after Jesus' baptism. But let's see what John says:

> *"The next day John saw Jesus coming toward him and said, "Look, the Lamb of God, who takes away the sin of the world!" (John 1:29)*

John, regarding the temptation of Jesus, utters not a single solitary word. John is resolute in his mind in regards to what takes place the following day and it completely differs from the other dude's respective accounts. The following day, John the Baptist announces to all and sundry that indeed Jesus is "the Son of God". Immediately thereafter, according to John, Jesus begins assembling his disciples. Problem being the other three have Jesus on day two of his forty-day temptation with the Devil in the desert.

Who is right and who is wrong? They can't all be right. In fact, I'd be willing to put my grandfather's war medals on them all being wrong. Nonetheless, if John is correct, the Synoptics are false, which places the spotlight of critical enquiry on their claims of credibility.

A further discrepancy is that the author of John, writes that John the Baptist did not know who Jesus was until after the baptism. But Matthew and Luke write that John the Baptist insisted that because he was beneath Jesus, then it should be Jesus doing the baptizing of him. As you can see it's not easy starting a new religion, a bookish religion, without the aid of fact checkers and editors… and with the absence of journalistic integrity.

Interesting Question

The following question has always troubled me. Why was it that if John the Baptist believed Jesus to be the Son of God, did *he* not become one of Jesus' followers or disciples? You would presume that if John the Baptist heard the voice of God say that Jesus was the 'chosen one', as written by the Gospels, then he would have dropped everything and followed the magic man wherever he went, but he didn't. Furthermore, most of John's disciples stayed loyal to *him*, and likewise chose not follow Jesus. In fact, John the Baptist had many followers, even centuries after his death. Why did they continue to follow John, instead of the prophesized Son of God?

Henceforth, we have an additional vast number of Jews who never met or heard of Jesus and who remained less than impressed with Christianity's Superman.

CHAPTER SEVEN

The Gospels on Jesus' Ministry

What Christians Know

Some time after being baptized by John in the Jordan River, and tempted by Satan in the Judean desert, Jesus is described as having left his hometown of Nazareth to begin the choosing of his disciples, and the commencement of his ministry. A ministry that, at its core, promised his second coming, a time that will usher in the Last Judgment of the living and the dead.

Christians are familiar with the idea that Jesus spoke in parables, metaphor, allegory, sayings, and proverbs. His most well known teachings, "Give no thought for the morrow", "Rich man", "Prodigal son", "He who is without sin", "Sower and the Seeds" and "Do unto others." Outside of this, however, your average Sunday Christian is a little hazy on the details, but we will cover these shortly.

The Joke

Jesus saw a crowd chasing down a woman to stone her and approached them. "What's going on here, anyway?" he asked.

"This woman was found committing adultery, and the law says we should stone her!" one of the crowd responded.

"Wait," yelled Jesus. "Let he who is without sin cast the first stone."

Suddenly, a stone was thrown from out of the sky, and knocked the woman on the side of her head.

"Aw, c'mon, Dad..." Jesus cried, "I'm trying to make a point here!"

How The Gospels Lied

Ok, in regards to the Length of Jesus' Ministry, here's a question that most twelve year old Sunday school students can answer: How long did Jesus' ministry last? Three years is the answer most often given, but is it correct? Well, according to John it is so. In his gospel, he includes the passing of three different Passover celebrations during the period between his baptism and his crucifixion. As the Passover is held only once per year, *ta-da*, we have our three years. So, yes Jesus' ministry lasts for three years according to John.

What of Matthew, Mark, and Luke? Do they mention three Passovers? No. Do they give any clue that it may have been three years? No, they don't. In fact, according to the Synoptic Gospels the duration of Jesus' ministry is not even twelve months. As a matter of fact, it's less than a few months. Admittedly, the Synoptic Gospels don't give an explicit time period but we calculate the duration from the passages within the scripture. Matthew, for example, lists the course of events leading up to commencement of Jesus' ministry, as the baptism; the temptation in the desert; the healing of a few; and finally the selection of the twelve disciples:

"After Jesus had finished instructing his twelve disciples, he went on from there to teach and preach in the towns of Galilee." (Matthew 11:1 NIV)

His ministry had begun, and what more or less follows immediately thereafter is the story of Jesus strolling through the cornfields on the Sabbath:

"His disciples were hungry and began to pick some ears of corn and eat them. When the Pharisees saw this, they said to him, 'Look! Your disciples are doing what is unlawful on the Sabbath." (Matthew 12:2-3 NIV)

We only need a 2nd grade education to understand that any locale more than 10 degrees north or south of the equator, one can only pick and eat the ears of the corn during the time of the harvest, which is the Fall. While it's fair to assume you already knew that, did you know that he was killed in the same year his ministry begun? Well, that is most certainly the case if we measure the series of events between the cornfield story and the execution. We also know that Jesus was killed on the day of the Passover, which is in the spring. Therefore, by reason of deduction we have reduced the duration of Jesus' ministry to only a few months.

Who's right – John? Or Matthew, Mark and Luke? Either one or three of them are selling it. Ultimately, it's your choice, but once you make that choice then whoever is shoveling the bullshit must be eliminated as a 'credible' source. Although I believe we have already discounted all four by process of elimination, but that's just me. You can decide for yourself.

THE CHOOSING OF THE TWELVE DISCIPLES

To be a bona fide Messiah, one of the first things you need in place is a fan base and thus Jesus' first order of business was to select disciples capable of recruiting and rallying new supporters. Matthew summarizes this entourage selection process in a neat and tidy two-paragraph verse.

> "As Jesus was walking beside the Sea of Galilee, he saw two brothers, Simon called Peter and his brother Andrew. They were casting a net into the lake, for they were fishermen. "Come, follow me," Jesus said, "and I will make you fishers of men." At once they left their nets and followed him. Going on from there, he saw two other brothers, James son of Zebedee and his brother John. They were in a boat with their father Zebedee, preparing their nets. Jesus called them, and immediately they left the boat and their father and followed him." (Matthew 4:18-22 NIV)

That's all it took for Jesus to convince the brothers to put down their rods, nets and follow this longhaired hippy who claimed to be from a town his disciples would had never heard of, Nazareth[*]. Mark writes in a similar vain to Matthew, but what does Luke have to say on the matter?

> *"One day as Jesus was standing by the Lake of Gennesaret, with the people crowding around him and listening to the word of God, he saw at the water's edge two boats, left there by the fishermen, who were washing their nets. He got into one of the boats, the one belonging to Simon, and asked him to put out a little from shore. Then he sat down and taught the people from the boat. When he had finished speaking, he said to Simon, "Put out into deep water, and let down the nets for a catch." Simon answered, "Master, we've worked hard all night and haven't caught anything. But because you say so, I will let down the nets."*
>
> *When they had done so, they caught such a large number of fish that their nets began to break. So they signaled their partners in the other boat to come and help them, and they came and filled both boats so full that they began to sink. When Simon Peter saw this, he fell at Jesus' knees and said, "Go away from me, Lord; I am a sinful man!" For he and all his companions were astonished at the catch of fish they had taken, and so were James and John, the sons of Zebedee, Simon's partners. Then Jesus said to Simon, "Don't be afraid; from now on you will catch men." So they pulled their boats up on shore, left everything and followed him." (Luke 5:1-11 NIV)*

---

[*] To this date, scholars and historians debate whether or not Nazareth was a real town during Jesus' time. Many contend that his Biblically claimed origins were penciled into fourth century manuscripts. This has a certain weight of credibility, as there is not a single mention of Nazareth outside of the New Testament until the early third century, when Sextus Julius Africanus, a Christian historian, speaks of "Nazara" as village in "Judea" and locates it near "Cochaba", a town still not identified by archaeologists today.

Joan Taylor, *Christians and the Holy Places*, writes: "It is now possible to conclude that there existed in Nazareth, from the first part of the fourth century, a small and unconventional church which encompassed a cave complex."

Luke's passage is completely at odds with his Synoptic contemporaries. By his account Jesus had asked Peter to take him out in his boat so that he can preach to the multitude. There is no multitude, or crowd present according to Matthew, or Mark. Further, the former Gospels have Jesus leaving the boat, but Luke has him entering a boat. What does John say?

> *"The next day, after the Baptism, John was there again with two of his disciples. When he saw Jesus passing by, he said, "Look, the Lamb of God!" When the two disciples heard him say this, they followed Jesus. Turning around, Jesus saw them following and asked, "What do you want?" They said, "Rabbi" "Where are you staying?" "Come," he replied, "and you will see." So they went and saw where he was staying, and spent that day with him. It was about the tenth hour. Andrew, Simon Peter's brother, was one of the two who heard what John had said and who had followed Jesus. The first thing Andrew did was to find his brother Simon and tell him, "We have found the Messiah" (that is, the Christ). And he brought him to Jesus. Jesus looked at him and said, "You are Simon son of John. You will be called Cephas" (which, when translated, is Peter." (John 1:35-42 NIV)*

By John's account it is Andrew who hears of Jesus via John the Baptist, and it was Andrew that went onto to recruit his brothers.

THE DIVINITY OF JESUS

As we have covered, John further distances himself from the Synoptic Gospels, in taking an enormous theological hammer in sculpting the divinity of Jesus. John is unabashedly brazen in his assertion that Jesus is God himself, that is - God in the human form. This is completely at odds with his contemporaries. John steps out swinging with this theological bombshell too, as the claim is made in the very first verse of his gospel:

"In the beginning was the Word, and the Word was with God, and the Word was God. He was God in the beginning." (John 1:1-2 NIV)

John doesn't stop there, he adds:

"Through him all things were made; without him nothing was made that has been made. In him was life, and that life was light of men." (John 1:3-4 NIV)

The language is a little tricky but the message is straightforward – Jesus was God. It is this passage that resulted in the founding church in Rome, the Catholic Church, getting all tongue-tied as they deliberated for centuries on the concept of the Trinity. It is a doctrine/dogma issue that still makes no sense to me. I mean if Jesus was God in the human form, then who was taking care of shit in Heaven while Jesus was alive? It's just illogical nonsense, but that's the beauty of religion; you can say whatever you like, and there'll always be people who are either bat-shit crazy or sufficiently gullible to believe such stupendous drivel!

If we compare John's bold assertion regarding the divinity of Jesus to the Synoptic Gospels, the difference couldn't be starker if it tried. On each occasion the other three make reference to Jesus by tacking on a title, it is as the 'Son of Man'. It is doubtful whether anyone could attach a more modest title, especially if he indeed was not the 'Son of Man' and instead the 'Son of God'.

Never, in a single instance does Matthew, Mark, or Luke within a bee's dick of making the same illustrious promise as John. And there is a really good reason for that; John had to make bigger and bolder claims about Jesus, because he was snookered behind the false prophecy promise of which the others had the luxury of writing still within the realms of the lifetime of the "current generation".

As we saw in chapter one, Jesus promised his return before his generation had *"tasted death."* Mark's Gospel, however, was still within range, albeit at the outer edge, of fulfilling that promise. John, however, writing at least two generations after Jesus' contemporaries had died - had to pour a little extra vodka into the party punch. He did this by proclaiming that Jesus was God himself. But big claims attract big attention!

JESUS THE APOCALYPTIC PROPHET

While we've already addressed the fact that Jesus preached about as an apocalyptic prophet, the 'end of times' was the quintessential message and resounding theme of Jesus' ministry throughout Matthew, Mark, and Luke. The message of 'end times coming' was basically that; judgment would follow; and the righteous would be rewarded with 24/7 harp music; and the evildoers cast aside into the bowels of hell for eternity.

> *"Whoever is ashamed of me and of my words in this adulterous and sinful generation, of that one will the Son of Man be ashamed when he comes in the glory of his Father with the holy angels…Truly I tell you, there are some standing here who will not taste death until they see the kingdom of God has come to power." (Mark 8:38-9:1 NIV)*

Jesus saw the world divided between the good and the bad. He, like John the Baptist, saw that the world was coming to an end because there was so much sin and evil in the world. They saw that the then current times mirrored the times of Sodom & Gomorrah and the chaotic and hedonistic times preceding the Flood, and naturally presumed that God's wrath would return.

Only this time, the good would be spared. Presumably, God learnt his lesson of painting everyone the same brush as he had during his earlier global genocides. Matthew and Luke claim as much in the following verse:

> *"For just as the flashing lightening lights up the earth from one part of the sky to the other, so will the Son of Man be in his day…And just as it was in the days of Noah, so will it*

be in the days of the Son of Man. They were eating,
drinking, marrying, and giving away in marriage, until the
day that Noah went into the ark and the flood came and
destroyed them all. So too will it be on the day when the
Son of Man is revealed." (Luke 17:24-27 NIV)

Moreover, Jesus not only promised all this would take
place during his contemporaries lifetime, but he also
hinted that it could take place on any day, at any minute.
Jesus preached that all his disciples and followers should
be prepared for the inevitable rapture:

"And you, be prepared, because you do not know the hour
when the Son of Man is coming." (Matthew 24:44 NIV)

Essentially, this was the essence of Jesus' much
proclaimed, "Take no thought for the morrow".
Christopher Hitchens writes in *God is Not Great:*

"This suggests – along with many other injunctions –
that things like thrift, innovation, family life, and so forth
are a sheer waste of time. This is why some of the Gospels,
canonical and apocryphal, report people (including Jesus'
family members) saying at the time that they thought
Jesus must be mad."

JESUS: LIAR, LUNATIC, OR LORD?

We have already put the liar accusation to bed, as Jesus is
quite obviously guilty as charged, but what of being a
lunatic?

Well, C.S Lewis certainly believed that if Jesus was not
God himself then the only suitable character judgment the
Bible leaves us with is that he was a sociopathic lunatic.
This is especially so because Jesus never calls himself God
in the gospels of Matthew, Mark, and Luke. Moreover, we
don't need to look too far to undercover many examples of
Jesus' apparent lunacy.

Case in point, the story found (only) in the Gospel of
John, regarding the woman caught committing adultery.

Interestingly, if you were to take a survey of Christians around the world there is little doubt that this narrative would be the most well known, at least outside of the nativity scene or the crucifixion.

This story is so celebrated by Christians, as many believe it portrays the wisdom and compassion of Jesus. A story so dear to the faithful that even the apparently Jew loathing Mel Gibson includes it, despite the scene being completely out of both context and order within the passion narrative, in his barely watchable and historically flawed *Passion of the Christ*.

The scene in question is the image of a woman dragged before Jesus and the Priests. The Pharisees ask Jesus should this adulterous woman be stoned to death in accordance with Mosaic Law. It is, of course, a trap set by the Pharisees, for if he agreed that she should be executed, he would have made nonsense of his own teachings of forgiveness and 'turn the other cheek'. On the other hand, if he didn't, then he was in violation of the Law and would have given the Pharisees reason to arrest him. Anyway, the Gospel John writes as such:

> "The teachers of the law and the Pharisees brought in a woman caught in adultery. They made her stand before the group and said to Jesus, "Teacher, this woman was caught in the act of adultery. In the Law Moses commanded us to stone such women. Now what do you say?" They were using this question as a trap, in order to have a basis for accusing him. But Jesus bent down and started to write on the ground with his finger. When they kept on questioning him, he straightened up and said to them, "If any one of you is without sin, let him be the first to throw a stone at her." Again he stooped down and wrote on the ground. At this, those who heard began to go away one at a time, the older ones first, until only Jesus was left, with the woman still standing there. Jesus straightened up and asked her, "Woman, where are they?

*Has no one condemned you?" "No one, sir," she said.
"Then neither do I condemn you," Jesus declared. "Go
now and leave your life of sin." (John 8:3-11)*

There are a myriad of philosophical issues and matters of
logic this passage presents:

1. Did Jesus just give his endorsement of sexual
   liberation and permissiveness? If so, then the Church
   has 2,000 years of sexual repression to answer for.
2. If the woman was caught in the act of intercourse,
   where was her accomplice, the husband?
3. The law of adultery applied only to a married
   woman, then what of her husband's justice? What
   punishment for the man that bonked his wife? The
   law demands, according to Leviticus, that he be
   put to death, along with her.
4. Did the woman ever sin again? Most likely she did,
   because she did got off Scot-free in this instance.
5. Matthew, for example, would never have written
   any passage like this, and he didn't, because this
   effectively has Jesus pissing on the pages of the
   Pentateuch. He would have been seen completely
   undermining the laws of Moses' as handed down
   directly by God. Jesus said quite clearly in
   Matthew, *"Anyone who breaks one of the least of these
   commandments and teaches others to do the same will be
   called least in the kingdom of heaven."*

Jesus may have danced around the philosophical trap set by
the Pharisees with some clever word play, but he
inadvertently leaves at least one aggrieved party suffering
and subsequently leaves us with more questions than
answers. Furthermore, this story was written into the
Gospel of John centuries later i.e. it was not written into the
original. We know this because the story is not found in our
oldest surviving manuscripts. Bart D. Ehrman, arguably the
world's current leading New Testament scholar, writes:

"(this story in John) includes a large number of words and phrases that are otherwise alien to the Gospel. The conclusion is unavoidable: this passage was not originally part of the Gospel."

Ultimately, you must make a decision; do you believe this event with the adulterous woman, given the above information, ever really took place? We know that whoever wrote John was most certainly not present at this event, as he wrote nearly 70 years after Jesus' death. We also know that it is inconsistent with Jesus' philosophy or theology as told by the other Synoptic Gospels. And we know this story to be added centuries later by some random dudes with their own motives. As such, the only conclusion we can draw is that this event simply never occurred.

THE GOLDEN RULE

"So whatever you wish that people would do to you, do so to them" (Matthew 7:12; Luke 6:31)

Oh the Golden Rule, and oh how Christians, for the most, believe this ethic for the promotion of human solidarity originated with their man, Jesus. Wrong!

"Hurt not others in ways that you yourself would find hurtful." – Buddha

"What stirs your anger when done to you by others, that do not to others." – Socrates

As you can see, the Golden Rule is far from unique to Jesus. In fact, Buddha and Socrates preceded Jesus by nearly 600 years. So not only is it fair to convict Jesus of false representation but it is evident that he had the artistic integrity of the fake 80's pop duo Milli Vanilli, who were dethroned when the tape player playing their music backstage in a concert malfunctioned… and as it turns out, they couldn't sing for so much so as a free supper!

Jesus is also credited with having been the originator of *"Love your neighbor as yourself" (Matthew 22:39; Mark 12:31;*

Luke 10:27) even though this was, in fact, taken from the Old Testament, Leviticus 19:18. In fact, the original Hebrew writing of Leviticus 19:18 is *"Love your fellow countrymen as yourself."* If you require further proof of God's xenophobic, racist philosophies - philosophies endorsed by Jesus - the commandment *"Thou shall not kill"* actually means *"Thou shall not kill a fellow Israelite, but slaughter away all others in your path."*

Despite all of the above, Jesus often strayed from his own god-damned rules. While he taught people should 'love their enemies' and 'turn the other cheek', he acted with a great deal of contempt towards those who disagreed with him. He displayed barely concealed hostility for his foreign neighbors, equating them to *"dogs"* and once instructing his disciples to *"go nowhere among the Gentiles"*. And as we reviewed in chapter one he even refused to heal a non-Jewish child, even though it was completely within his power and discretion, because he declared that he was here only to heal the *"lost sheep of Israel"*.

Furthermore, Jesus spoke out specifically against anger. Specifically in Matthew:

> *"Anyone who is angry with his brother shall be liable to judgment"* (Matthew 5:22)

Compare that, however, to this passage in Luke:

> *"If anyone comes to me and does not hate his father and mother, his wife and children, his brothers and sisters — yes, even his own life — he cannot be my disciple."*
> (Luke 14:26 NIV)

Either, Jesus was completely bi-polar (not a gay bear) or he was the poster boy for the astrological sign Gemini. The duality of personality portrayed by these writers could not be starker.

The Triumphant Return to Jerusalem: This narrative is the doozy of doozies, and one that I'd bet Matthew is still rolling in his grave over, having made such a glaring balls-up of interpreting the Hebrew language, as written in the Old Testament. Remember that Mark was the first of the Gospels to write of Jesus, and Matthew, and Luke copied much of Mark's work some 15-20 years later.

Mark writes:

"When they brought the colt to Jesus and threw their cloaks over it, he sat on it." (11:7)

Luke writes:

"They brought it to Jesus, threw their cloaks on the colt and put Jesus on it." (14:26)

What does Matthew write? Well, Matthew with his determination to link everything about Jesus back to the Old Testament prophets, writes:

"Say to the Daughter of Zion, 'See, your king comes to you, gentle and riding on a donkey, on a colt, the foal of a donkey." (Matthew 21:5)

Matthew quotes the above passage directly from the prophet Zechariah verse 9:9 so as to further match the events of Jesus' life to the Hebrew Bible. What Matthew doesn't seem to realize though, is that the verse in question from Zechariah is a Hebrew poem, and the word *'and'* was used to give emphasis, in what is termed 'synonymous parallelism'. Matthew's Greek mother tongue misses that poetry all together and we have the comical scene of imagining Jesus riding simultaneously on a horse and a donkey. I ask you this, how triumphant can any man look, including John Wayne, riding into town with one leg draped over an ass and the other over a horse? "Whoa there horsey, whoa there donkey. I am the Son of Man whoa wait a minute folks, sit donkey. Stay horsey!"

JESUS WAS AN ANGRY BASTARD

Meek and mild or short-tempered and foul mouthed? Well, once again, it depends which of the Gospel accounts you're reading from. That said, since Mark forms the basis for Matthew, and Luke and John is completely bloody well made up, we can argue, most certainly, that Jesus got around with a short wick. [Insert your own joke here]

Mark had the disadvantage of not having his writing checked for theological flaws, whereas Matthew and Luke had the benefit of ironing out the chinks. Jesus' short temper was indeed a problematic concern for the latter writers. A terrific example of this is when we examine the story of the old man being healed by Jesus inside the synagogue on the Sabbath. Mark writes:

> "He looked around at them **in anger** and, deeply distressed at their stubborn hearts said to the man, "Stretch out your hand." He stretched it out, and his hand was completely restored." (Mark 3:5 NIV)

Now compare Mark's passage with Luke's:

> "He looked around at them all, and then said to the man, "Stretch out your hand." He did so, and his hand was completely restored." (Luke 6:10 NIV)

Not once does Matthew or Luke write of Jesus being angry. There are many examples whereby Matthew or Luke tells of the same narrative word for word, except for the removal of any word that displayed Jesus as an angry man.

Another example of Jesus' petulance is in comparing Mark and Matthew on the story of Jesus' anger with his disciples for not allowing the children to be brought to him to be blessed:

> "When Jesus saw this, he was **indignant**. He said to them, "Let the little children come to me, and do not hinder them, for the kingdom of God belongs to such as these." (Mark 10:14 NIV)

Matthew makes the omission of the entire uncomplimentary first sentence, one that obviously caused him some embarrassment:

> *"Jesus said, "Let the little children come to me, and do not hinder them, for the kingdom of heaven belongs to such as these." (Matthew 19:14 NIV)*

Christians are often quick to call me 'petty' for such citations, but we have such slim pickings to read over in attempting to paint a proper picture of Jesus, that these small points all add up. They do not add up in favor for those who think he was the softly spoken fisher of men.

Would it be possible for someone truly meek and mild mannered to run through the Temple grounds yelling and tossing merchant and moneychanger's tables over, as Jesus did? Of course not, one must have a fiery disposition to do such a thing. I consider myself mild mannered, and while I've felt some distress strolling past GOP volunteers handing out 'How to Vote for Sarah Palin' cards, I've never run into their headquarters to toss their furniture all about the place, as such I respect their right to free speech to do such a thing. But that doesn't stop me fantasizing about doing just that. Every. Goddamn. Day.

JESUS AS A MORAL TEACHER

This leads to the question - was Jesus a great moral teacher, a role model for moral perfection? This is ultimately a difficult standard for any human to attain, but we are led to believe, by our church leaders, that Jesus absolutely was a fantastic example of moral perfection.

Philosophers contend that "great ethical or moral teachers" commonly develop full and coherent ethical systems that provide a comprehensive basis for illuminating ethical attitudes and behavior. Does this definition marry up with Jesus' teachings? Well, a read of the Bible leaves us with no such blue print. Instead we find a mish-mash of homilies and pronouncements, indecipherable parables, double entendres, cryptic prophecies - some of which are unclear and others of which are outright contradictory or hypocritical. With his love for babbling on and the fact he was only about 4'7" – I am sure this is the origin of the phrase "small talk".

Surprisingly though, even non-Christians also choose to believe he was a great moral teacher. I presume this to be the case because they've either not read the New Testament, or they've just read it with an uncritical eye. In fact, I have friends that don't believe Jesus was God, or the Son of God, but still consider themselves Christians due to what they believe were His great moral philosophies. This cut and paste perspective is obviously contrary to the Gospels message, however. Faith is a tremendous beta-blocker for rationality.

The New Testament demands that you believe unequivocally that Jesus died for our sins; that He rose from death on the third day; and you must accept him as your Savior. Therein lays the durability of religion though; people can pick and choose what they want to believe – even if their beliefs are counter to the pivotal character's message. I believe that attitude is purely borne out of ignorance of what is written in the text. But many brilliant men and women have argued for the affirmative, including the greatest of the founding fathers, Thomas Jefferson, who published the Jefferson Bible in the early 1800s.

Jefferson wasn't a big fan of all the hocus-pocus nonsense that was created by the Christian church, so he stripped away all the supernatural references contained in the New Testament. Out went the virgin birth. Gone were the miracles; the walking on water, the feeding of the 5,000, and the raising from the dead. Jefferson kept only Jesus' moral teachings, which he called "the most sublime and benevolent code of morals which has ever been offered to man." As a figure of historical importance I rate Jefferson extremely high, but this was one of his lowest moments, in my honest opinion. Let's now examine the evidence.

A careful read of the New Testament reveals that, in fact, his actual behavior and philosophies fall terribly short of the idolized and glorified image that our Pastors, Priests, Elders, Deacons, Reverends, Evangelicals, Ministers, and even Thomas Jefferson spew forth. For example, he made it known in no uncertain terms that anyone that didn't embrace his teachings would be subject to the most heinous of punishments, eternal torture in Hell.

Socrates and Buddha taught almost identical fundamental values, but neither of Jesus' theological rivals said, "You better listen to me or your anus will be reamed with a white hot rod of steel for the next trillion gazillion years." This is far from a message of love, mercy, compassion, and solidarity, isn't it? Yes, it is!

Jesus repeatedly prophesized doom, division, and destruction to anyone, or any nation, that rejects his ministry. Here Jesus gives is orders to his disciples:

"But when you enter a town and are not welcomed, go into its streets and say, 'Even the dust of your town that sticks to our feet we wipe off against you. Yet be sure of this: The kingdom of God is near.' I tell you, it will be more bearable on that day for Sodom than for that town." (Luke 10:10-12 NIV)

In the event that the message is not loud and clear, Jesus adds a little more fire and brimstone:

"Woe to you, Korazin! Woe to you, Bethsaida! For if the miracles that were performed in you had been performed in Tyre and Sidon, they would have repented long ago, sitting in sackcloth and ashes. But it will be more bearable for Tyre and Sidon at the judgment than for you. And you, Capernaum, will you be lifted up to the skies? No, you will go down to the depths." (Luke 10:13-15 NIV)

Does all of this give you the slightest impression that Jesus was a nice guy? If that doesn't convince you then possibly you need to consider that it was Jesus who introduced us to the concepts of eternal damnation and torture in perpetuity. A doctrine that demands infinite punishment for a finite sin i.e. you sin for forty years but you're tortured for eternity.

Close your eyes and picture how long eternity it is. It's forever. Go out a trillion years, and then add another trillion years, and another, and so on and so on. It is impossible to ponder such infinity with our finite little minds, complex and evolved as they are.

Prior to Jesus entering the scene, and prior to the arrival of the New Testament, man had a pretty rudimentary life. He was born, he'd work his fields, tend to his flock in a hot, dusty, dry desert climate, without SPF 50+ or lip balm, only to return to his non-air-conditioned mud hut each evening for a sit down course of manna bread. It is, without a doubt, certainly a miserable standard of living by our twenty-first century standards, but at least at the end of this hard slog somewhere on the Arabian Peninsula, your suffering ended the moment death descended upon you.

Peace at last in the shade, deep in your own grave. There was no going to heaven or hell in the passages of the Old Testament (as in Jewish tradition you die and you're dead... pretty sensible, right?). But then Jesus comes along and says, *"Wait a minute. No, that's all wrong. If you don't believe what I have to say then you're suffering has only just begun at the moment of death."*

It's an utterly repugnant and morally despicable doctrine for anyone to preach. 'Do what I say or else!' This was the cornerstone of Jesus' ministry. The promise that the rapture would come and divide the good, defined as followers, from the bad, defined as doubters, in the respective celestial destinations of heaven and hell. The reasons for my distaste for Jesus far from ends here, for everything he said or did which was nice or good, he said or did 10 things to the bloody contrary! He even says as much himself:

> *"Do you think I came to bring peace on earth? No, I tell you, but division. From now on there will be five in one family divided against each other, three against two and two against three. They will be divided, father against son and son against father, mother against daughter and daughter against mother, mother-in-law against daughter-in-law and daughter-in-law against mother-in-law."* (Luke 12:50-53 NIV)

This is directly at odds with the Old Testament's overarching commandment to honor thy parents. It is also of more concern that it resembles the creeds of personality cults that demand abandonment of one's family, so as to give oneself totally to the subservience of the leader.

Please don't think these are obscure passages, because they are most certainly not. One such passage in Luke really portrays Jesus as a megalomaniac monster; when Jesus commands a man to follow him and the man agrees but requests that he have time to prepare a funeral for his deceased father, whom he still mourned for. Jesus replied curtly:

> *"Let the dead bury their own dead, but you go and proclaim the kingdom of God."* (Luke 9:60 NIV)

Similarly, another man accepted Jesus' invitation to follow him but the man pleaded, "I will follow you, Lord; but first let me go back and say good-by to my family." Jesus, again, grunted forth:

> *"No one who puts his hand to the plow and looks back is fit for service in the kingdom of God."* (Luke 9:62)

As you can plainly see, there is no evidence of Jesus representing even an ethical model for good family values. While Jesus was fond of endorsing the Old Testament commandment to 'Honor thy father and thy mother', he in fact treated his mother terribly on more than a few occasions.

Jesus, age 12, gave his mother a verbal dressing-down for having the nerve to look for him at the Temple. *"How is it that you sought me? Did you not know that I had to be in my Father's house?"* Mind you, this was after he had been missing for three days.

Then on another occasion, his mother and brothers came to see him give one of his sermons. One of Jesus' disciples spotted his family in the crowd, and interrupted Jesus, *"My Lord your mother and brothers are here, and they want to speak to you."* To which Jesus replied,

> *"Who is my mother, and who are my brothers?"* Pointing
> to his disciples, he said, *"Here are my mother and my
> brothers. For whoever does the will of my Father in
> heaven is my brother and sister and mother."*
> (Matthew 12:48-50 NIV)

Seems Jesus didn't quite honor his mother's immaculate conception nearly as much as the Vatican does. Somewhat comically, Mark suggests that Jesus' family thought he was but a raving mad man:

> *"Then Jesus entered a house, and again a crowd gathered,
> so that he and his disciples were not even able to eat.
> When his family heard about this, they went to take
> charge of him, for they said, "He is out of his mind."*
> (Mark 3:20-21 NIV)

This passage yet a further example of a point made earlier, that despite God foretelling Mary, according to Luke, that she would bear his child, everything Jesus says or does comes as a complete surprise to her. In my opinion, this is further evidence that because Matthew and Luke copied their accounts from Mark, their inclusion of the virgin birth story forced them to maintain a supporting storyline.

DEMANDED HIS ENEMIES KILLED

"But those enemies of mine who did not want me to be king over them – bring them here and kill them in front of me." (Luke 19:27 NIV)

This was Jesus talking to his disciples, directing them to take action against those Jewish citizens that denied Jesus was king. It also echoes Matthews' account of Jesus, saying:

"He who is not with me is against me"

Here's a better idea, Jesus, why don't you try being a little more convincing in your claim that you are indeed king, or Messiah, so that we are not left with 38,000 denominations of Christianity, and hundreds of religious faiths that cover the globe? Isn't this of sounder mind than just killing those that fall short of being convinced?

Of course, in retrospection, we know the answer to this: crusades, inquisition, witch trials, Hitler's Nazis "doing the work of the creator", Stalin being endorsed by the Russian Orthodox Church. Throughout recorded history, we have many examples of 'faithful' people taking up Jesus' charge and putting those who would not capitulate, to the sword… or gun… or a-bomb,

The problem of contradiction remains the same, however, as Jesus, in Luke's passage, condemns his enemies to death, but then Matthew quotes Jesus as having said:

"You have heard that it was said, 'Love your neighbor and hate your enemy.' But I tell you: Love your enemies and pray for those who persecute you." (Matthew 5:43-44 NIV)

Do we love them or do we kill our enemies, bi-polar-Jesus? The New Testament leaves us with no discernible conclusion, yet again.

Ultimately, the ministry of Jesus provides 21st century man with no further illumination of the human condition than what any other book from antiquity could or can provide.

Jesus Didn't Love His Enemies, Why Should We?

Jesus told us to 'love our enemies' but how is this practical? How are we to love Islamo-fascists who will not rest until we infidels have been converted, conquered, or liberated of our heads? Sure, it's a 'nice' thing to say but even Jesus couldn't follow his own advice, regularly referring to his doubters as *"brood of vipers"*, *"hypocrites"* or worse, imparting the threat of fiery damnation for eternity. Furthermore, what advice from Jesus' teachings can we take from the Gospels that could help mankind deal with the complicated social problems that face our world today, such as racial, ethnic, and sexual discrimination; slavery; managing the environment; the death penalty; slavery; economic justice; human cloning, and ethical governing standards? There is nothing... well, that's not true, we could just take Jesus' advice and kill everything that doesn't capitulate to 'our way'.

What of slavery? What did Jesus have to say in regards to arguably the biggest blight on western civilization's experience in the last 2000 years? Nothing! He was absolutely silent on the issue, despite the practice of slavery being widespread throughout the Roman Empire during his time.

Instead, when the subject of slavery did come up, Jesus let it be known, that he believed a *"slave should serve his master"*. Imagine how many lives and how much suffering would have never occurred in America alone had Jesus denounced slavery. At least 618,000 lives wouldn't have been cut short during the American Civil War alone.

Differing Teaching Styles

Every teacher has his or her own unique style - some are authoritative, others are collaborative, whereas others still prefer to give direct answers, and some prefer to lead their students along the path to knowledge with well placed clues. The Gospels, however, leave us with the impression that Jesus was completely arbitrary, blatantly impetuous, flighty, and schizophrenic. The difference, of teaching styles, is best illustrated between the contrast of Mark and John's gospel. Barry Qualls, in his essay, '*Saint Mark Says They Mustn't*', writes:

> "*His (Mark's) Son of God is always in crowds and always seeking an isolated place, always speaking and yet urging silence, always explaining and yet certain his words will not be understood. His family, who enter the text without introduction, are amazed by his denial of them (3:31-35); his friends are certain "he is beside himself" (3:21) and his enemies, not surprisingly, echo these responses and add others. The disciples question, "what manner of man is this" from early on (4:41) and are repeatedly "astonished at his words", questioning what such use of language signifies.*"

This is as good a one-paragraph-summary of the Gospel of Mark as you will ever find. In fact all three of the Synoptic Gospels present Jesus as both evasive and secretive with regards to his identity. Now, if we examine John's gospel, we find a complete contrast, and the author comes out swinging in the opening verse:

> "*In the beginning was the Word, and the Word was with God, and the Word was God. He was God in the beginning.*" (John 1:1-2 NIV)

There is no mystery with Jesus' ministry according to John. Jesus is not secretive or evasive, he is completely forthright and therefore teaches in such manner. An illustration of this is in chapter eight of John, whereby Jesus is conversing with the Pharisees:

> "*Your Father Abraham rejoiced that he was to see my day; he saw it was glad.*" The Jews then said to Jesus, "*You are not yet fifty years of old, and have you seen Abraham?*" Jesus said to them, "*Truly, truly, truly, I say to you, before Abraham was, I am.*" (John 8:56-58 NIV)

This is John portraying a boastful Jesus, *"I am greater than Abraham"* which by default implies him greater than the Jewish hero Moses. In other words, *"Listen here Jews! Stop following Moses, your new Deliverer is here!"*

Ultimately, Christians revere Jesus' teachings not because they're profoundly extraordinary or uniquely spectacular. Simply, they award His teachings praise and accolades because of their source, Jesus. Moreover, by the very nature that so few people actually read or comprehend the New Testament, His words have been given a certain degree of loftiness. Most significantly, this is counter with the understanding we have of moral principles, insofar as moral behavior should be evaluated on its own, regardless of who might have formulated them.

CHAPTER EIGHT

The Gospels on Jesus' Miracles

What Christians Know

If you don't know at least a handful of Jesus alleged miracles then it is doubtful you ever attended a single church sermon or a Sunday school class. I guess everyone in the Western World is familiar with; water into wine; walking on water; raising Lazarus; the feeding of the 5,000; healing a blind man; healing a leper.

These are stories we know verbatim, and stories that Christians accept as sacrosanct. They also prove that the dividing line between theists and atheists is belief in the suspension and circumvention of the laws governing nature.

The Joke

A religious man is on top of a roof during a great flood. A man comes by in a boat and says "get in, get in!" The religious man replies, "no I have faith in God, he will grant me a miracle."

Later the water is up to his waist and another boat comes by and the guy tells him to get in again. He responds that he has faith in God and that God will deliver him a miracle. With the water at about chest height, another boat comes to rescue him, but he turns down the offer again cause "God will grant me a miracle."

With the water at chin height, a helicopter throws down a ladder and they tell him to get in, mumbling with the water in his mouth, he again turns down the request for help for the faith of God. He arrives at the gates of heaven with broken faith and says to Peter, I thought God would grand me a miracle and I have been let down." St. Peter chuckles and responds, "I don't know what you're complaining about, we sent you three boats and a helicopter."

How The Gospels Lied

Did Jesus perform miracles as a means to relieve suffering or were his bag of miraculous magic tricks signs of his divinity? Again, the answer depends on which Gospel you are reading. By sheer volume, of Mark's 661 verses, approximately 200, or one-third, have Jesus performing various miracles.

The author goes to great literary lengths to present Jesus as a profound humanitarian. He hungers, groans, prays, fears, urges, and several times, grows angry and fatigued. Matthew and Luke, copying from Mark, visibly share this view of Jesus. Therefore, via the Synoptic Gospels we read of incidents where Jesus heals a blind person, a leper, and the demonically possessed. In other words, the viewpoint of the three Synoptic Gospels is that Jesus performed miracles for the sole intention of helping the downtrodden and unfortunate.

There are a dozen or so examples whereby Jesus is asked to perform a miracle to prove he is who he and others claim he is, and responds so with a ferocious outburst. For example, there is a passage in Matthew where some Jewish elders, including the Pharisees ask Jesus:

"Teacher, we want to see a miraculous sign from you."
(Matthew 12:38 NIV)

Jesus' replies with great fury:

"A wicked and adulterous generation asks for a
miraculous sign! But none will be given it except the sign
of the prophet Jonah. For as Jonah was three days and
three nights in the belly of a huge fish, so the Son of Man

will be three days and three nights in the heart of the
earth." (Matthew 12:39-40 NIV)

In other words, Jesus proclaims that he will never use a miracle as a tool for proving his majesty. The Jonah metaphor is a nice little cryptic clue, as it is his only allusion to his future resurrection three days after his death, as with the case of the prophet Jonah. How delightfully devilish of Jesus!

There is also the passage in Matthew where Jesus is on his 40 day tease-a-thon with Satan. The red skinned horned devil took Jesus to the top of the Temple in Jerusalem, with the offer that if Jesus should jump (because surely his father, God, would save him) then, in return, he would give him the keys to the kingdom of earth:

"If you are the Son of God," the Devil said, "Then throw
yourself down. For it is written: "He will command his
angels concerning you, and they will lift you up in their
hands, so that you will not strike your foot against a
stone." (Matthew 4:6 NIV)

Jesus considered the offer for only a nanosecond before replying forcefully:

"It is also written: 'Do not put the Lord your God to the
test." (Matthew 4:7 NIV)

So, whatever you do, don't ask God to prove his existence by way of asking FOR ANYTHING during prayer. I.e. forget *'Ask and ye shall receive'*. I digress.

It's interesting to note that this is a line taken directly from the Hebrew Bible, verses 6:16 of Deuteronomy. As you can see, the Synoptic Gospels are quick to point out the purpose and limitations of Jesus' miracles.

This viewpoint, however, is not shared with John, who calls the miraculous performances of Jesus 'signs', rather than miracles. These 'signs', according to John, are used explicitly for the purpose of convincing people to worship him as God.

Case in point, Jesus revisited the city of Cana in Galilee, the same town he performed the water into wine trick at a wedding reception, there was a royal official whose son was suffering some mystery illness. The illness is unknown but John writes that the young boy was on his 'deathbed.' The official learns of Jesus' whereabouts, and having heard of his majesty and miracles, summons Jesus to his home to heal his son. After arriving (without so much as a cake or casserole, mind you), Jesus says:

"Unless you people see miraculous signs and wonders,
you will never believe in me." (John 4:48 NIV)

Jesus lays his hands on the boy's head, and says to his father:

"You may go. Your son will live."

Jesus departs, and seven hours later the boy's health is miraculously restored. This is one of seven 'signs' of John's gospel, with the most famous being the resurrection of Lazarus, a story unique to John.

Lazarus was from Bethlehem and was in the final throes of battling some kind of terminal illness. The dying man's sister sent for Jesus in hopes of a divine intervention to save her brother's life. Jesus receives the telegram, reads it and replies, *"Do not worry your brother's life will not end in death"*, but he decides to stay where he is to continue his preaching. A few days later Jesus finally turns up to their house, but is informed that Lazarus has been dead in his tomb the past four days. The dead man's sister scolds Jesus, *"Lord if you had been here when we sent for you, my brother would still be alive."* Jesus calms the grieving sibling with the words:

"Your brother will rise again. I am the resurrection and
the life. He who believes in me will live, even though he
dies; and whoever lives and believes in me will never die.
Do you believe this?" (John 11: 23-26 NIV)

JESUS LIED – HE WAS ONLY HUMAN

The woman replies, *"Yes I do believe this"*, and in turn Jesus asks to be led to the deceased's tomb. Once there, the accompanying relatives of Lazarus forewarn him of the odor that will most likely be emanating from the rotting corpse. Jesus rolls away the stone guarding the tomb with his great big god like arms, and plants himself next to the dead Lazarus. Jesus then closes his eyes, tilts his head skywards, and calls out to God:

> *"Father, I thank you that you have heard me. I knew that you always hear me, but I said this for the benefit of the people standing here, that they may believe that you sent me." (John 11:41-42 NIV)*

I wonder how it was that Lazarus' sister repaid Jesus. Seriously, nothing gets the ladies jumping like turning their dead brother into a freaking zombie! So I am told.

Nonetheless, this passage further illustrates that John believed the purpose of Jesus' miracles were divine signs specifically crafted to make the disbelieving rabble of people believe in him. Of course, being the devout believer that I am, I really shouldn't point out that John's testament of Jesus' 'signs' completely contradicts the accounts of the other Synoptic Gospels.

A further theological hole that John digs for himself by means of this passage is in that he records Jesus asking his heavenly father for his prayer to be answered. But John states clearly that unlike the others, Jesus is God in the human form. Why would Jesus then need to pray to himself for miraculous intervention for the resurrection of Lazarus, which he could easily perform himself? It makes no sense whatsoever, mind you, maybe I shouldn't be so picky… most of John makes no sense… brings in lots of dollars though. And keeps the guy with the John 3:16 sign at football games in a job!

From a historicity perspective, like everything else that has been alleged to have happened during Jesus' life, no external accounts or reports of these supposed miracles exist. G. A. Wells, observes in his book, *The Historical Evidence of Jesus:*

> *"Their (Gospels) miracle stories are nearly all couched in general terms, with no indication of time or place or details concerning the person or persons who benefited."*

What I personally find troubling, at least from a philosophical standpoint, is that Jesus is claimed by the Gospels to be either the Son of God, or God himself. If this is so, then surely it's only reasonable to enquire as to why he used his miraculous gift of curing illness or benefiting mankind in such an astonishingly limited fashion.

Jesus healed a blind man but not blindness; he healed a leper but not leprosy. Biblical analysis points to the fact the he only ever healed a small group of Palestinians living in a tiny little part of the Mediterranean. Is it too much to expect that such a divine being with insight, apparently, far beyond even our earthly imaginations, should have provided us more?

If John is right, and miracles were a tool to prove his divine status, then why are we left with so much doubt? Obviously, the writers of the New Testament had only a 2nd century understanding of science and medicine (ah, she has a temperature, we should trepan her skull – Google 'trepanning'!), and therefore, as an obvious piece of fiction, their lead character, Jesus is saddled with their limited imagination and creativity.

Another former minister turned non-Christian is Charles Templeton who tackles the issue of the Gospels' claims for the miraculous in his book, *Farewell to God: My reasons for rejecting the Christian faith:*

> *"Most of the illnesses that afflict humans were beyond the comprehension of the men and women of that day and, of course, beyond Jesus' comprehension, too. No one at that point in history had even a rudimentary understanding of*

the causes of physiological or psychological illnesses or of the various other afflictions to which humankind is subject. Most thought of them as punishments from God or the machinations of Satan or other evil spirits.

"When, for instance, epilepsy brought on a seizure that caused the victim to collapse and writhe on the ground as though struggling with an internal enemy, when food poisoning produced a paroxysm of vomiting, when a raging fever led to intense shivering and delirium, or when a migraine attack produced visual aberrations and excruciating pain, it seemed reasonable in that pre-scientific time to interpret such phenomena as the work of an evil spirit. And, when the affliction passed, it was equally reasonable to interpret it as the triumph of a benign spirit over a malign.

"Many illnesses, then as now, were psychosomatic and could be 'cured' when the sufferer's perception changed. Just as today a placebo prescribed by a physician in whom the patient has faith can effect an apparent cure, so, in earlier time, faith in the healer could banish adverse symptoms. With each success the healer's reputation would grow and his powers would, as a consequence, become more efficacious. It would appear evident that this is what happened with Jesus . . .It is clear in the text that Jesus was seen by the general populace as a wonder-worker. The stories of his exploits were before him--by word of mouth, of course, and thus subject to embellishing--and when he entered a town the state of heightened expectation would often be close to mass hysteria. As a consequence, the apparently miraculous would happen." (Templeton, pp. 111-112)

Jesus' Miracles

A summary of each of Jesus' thirty-four miracles, as recorded by the respective Gospels, include:

1. Water into wine *(John)*
2. Healing of the Royal official's son in Capernaum *(John)*
3. Healing of the demonically possessed man in Capernaum *(Mark and Luke)*
4. Healing of Peter's mother in law *(Matthew, Mark and Luke)*
5. Catching a vast number of fish in Simon's boat *(Luke)*
6. Healing a leper *(Matthew and Mark)*
7. Healing a Centurion's servant *(Matthew and Luke)*
8. Healing a paralytic *(Matthew, Mark and Luke)*
9. Healing a withered hand *(Matthew and Mark)*
10. Raising a widow's son *(Luke)*
11. Calming the stormy sea *(Matthew, Mark and Luke)*
12. Healing the demonically possessed woman in Gerasene *(Matthew, Mark and Luke)*
13. Healing a woman with internal bleeding *(Matthew, Mark and Luke)*
14. Raising Jairus' daughter *(Matthew, Mark and Luke)*
15. Healing two blind men *(Matthew)*
16. Healing a mute that was demonically possessed *(Matthew)*
17. Healing a 38 year old invalid *(John)*
18. The feeding of 5000 men *(Matthew, Mark, Luke and John)*
19. Walking on water *(Matthew, Mark and John)*
20. Healing a demonically possessed girl in Tyre *(Matthew and Mark)*
21. Healing a deaf man with a speech impediment *(Mark)*
22. The feeding of 4000 men *(Matthew and Mark)*

23. Healing a blind man Bethsaida *(Mark)*
24. Healing a man born blind *(John)*
25. Healing a demonically possessed boy *(Matthew, Mark and Luke)*
26. Catching a fish with a coin in its mouth *(Matthew)*
27. Healing a blind and demonically possessed man *(Matthew and Luke)*
28. Healing a woman that had been crippled for 18 years *(Luke)*
29. Healing a man with dropsy *(Luke)*
30. Healing ten lepers *(Luke)*
31. Raising of Lazarus *(John)*
32. Healing of Bartimaeus of blindness *(Mark)*
33. Restoring a severed ear *(Luke)*
34. Catching a great number of fish *(John)*

In summary, of the thirty-four documented miracles – only one 'miraculous event' is recorded by all four Gospels; the feeding of 5000 men. Sixteen of thirty-four are recorded by only one of the four.

A Christian must now ask himself one or two confronting questions, such as why would, for example, three of the Gospels include the account of Jesus walking on water, which let's face it – must have been fucking incredible – but Luke decided it was irrelevant to his biography? Hmm.

The bigger question for me, however, is considering that the proclaimed Son of God is said to have spent the best part of thirty-five years on earth, what did he really accomplish in that time? Six of his thirty-four miracles were wasted on healing people that he believed were possessed by demons. An illness mistakenly diagnosed for centuries until Louis Pasteur discovered the Germ Theory for disease. Which means, effectively, that Jesus spent 15% of his magical powers on healing people with, most likely, the common cold. It really is an absurd notion that the spawn of the Prime Mover would have no knowledge of bacteria.

Philosopher David Hume argued against the plausibility of miracles in framing the argument into four concise points:

1. A miracle is a violation of the known laws of nature.
2. We know these laws through repeated and constant experience.
3. The testimony of those who report miracles contradicts the operation of known scientific laws.
4. Consequently no one can rationally believe in miracles.

In regards to point 4, that is unless, of course, you lack intellectual curiosity and critical thinking skills. Or suffer long term brain damage from a horrific waterskiing accident involving a telegraph pole positioned a little too close to the water's edge.

Voltaire, the eighteenth century French enlightenment philosopher, Voltaire, illuminated the vast number of religiously claimed miracles, miracles that are shared across neighboring faiths, when he wrote in *Miracles and Idolatry*:

"The daughters of the high priest Anius changed whatever they chose into wheat, wine or oil. Athaldia, daughter of Mercury, was resurrected several times. Aesculapius resuscitated Hippolytus. Hercules dragged Alcestis back from the death. Heres returned to the world after passing a fortnight in hell. The parents of Romulus and Remus were a god and a vestal virgin. The Palladium fell from heaven in the city of Troy. The hair of Berenice became a constellation....Give me the name of one people among whom incredible prodigies were not performed, especially when few knew how to read or write."

It's pertinent to point out that the age of miracles died when the last of the prophets and sages died more than millennia ago and before the advent of 24/7 cable newswires. We simply don't witness the suspension of nature anymore. That all ceased with the invention of recording equipment such as cameras. Put in another way, the camera killed your god!

The Odds That You Witnessed a Miracle

Christopher Hitchens examines the probability that what you believed you witnessed actually did defy the laws of nature:

> *"A miracle is a disturbance or interruption in the expected and established course of things. If you seem to witness such a thing, there are two possibilities. The first is that the law of nature have been suspended (in your favor). The second is that you are under a misapprehension, or suffering from a delusion. Thus the likelihood of the second must be weighted against the first.*

> *If you only hear a report of the miracle from a second or third party, the odds must be adjusted accordingly before you can decide to credit a witness who claims to have seen something that you did not see. And if you are separated by from the "sighting" by many generations, and have no independent corroboration, the odds must be adjusted still more drastically."*

CHAPTER NINE

The Gospels on Jesus' Arrest

What Christians Know

The arrest of Jesus is a pivotal event in the Gospels, as it ultimately leads to the crucifixion and resurrection, and, at least on the surface, it's a well-known story. In Christian theology, the events from the Last Supper until the death and resurrection of Jesus are referred to as The Passion.

Most know that Jesus had instructed his disciples to prepare a meal for the Passover, a meal that is now referred to as the Last Supper. This final meal was the last Jesus would share with his dozen followers. In an act of betrayal by his beloved Judas Iscariot, an act prophesized by Jesus during the Last Supper, the Roman soldiers and Jewish Priests are led to the Garden of Gethsemane where Jesus and his men have camped for the evening.

The Joke

Every year, just before Easter, the Chief Rabbi in Rome goes to the Vatican and presents an ancient, and by now quite tattered envelope to the Pope. The Pope inspects the envelope, shakes his head, and hands it back to the Chief Rabbi, who then departs.

This has been going on for nearly two thousand years. One year recently, it happened that there was a new Pope and a new Chief Rabbi. When the Chief Rabbi presented the ancient envelope to the Pope, as he had been instructed to do by his predecessor, the Pope looked it over and handed it back as he had been told to, in turn, by his predecessor ... but then the Pope said, "This is an unusual ritual. I don't understand it. What is in this envelope?"

"Damned if I know," answered the Chief Rabbi. "I'm new here myself. But, hey, let's open it and find out."

"Good idea," said the Pope. So together, they slowly and carefully opened the envelope. And do you know what they found? The caterer's bill for the Last Supper!

How The Gospels Lied

The Synoptic Gospels report that Jesus predicted his execution on several occasions throughout the course of their respective writings. The first time we learn of this prediction is in chapter eight of Mark:

> *"He then began to teach them that the Son of Man must suffer many things and be rejected by the elders, chief priests and teachers of the law, and that he must be killed and after three days rise again. He spoke plainly about this." (Mark 8:31-32 NIV)*

The final sentence of this passage is an interesting choice of words. It implies that Jesus "spoke plainly" about his impending doom, suggesting he is not only comfortable with the idea but also understanding of the meaning of his death. Moreover, Jesus uses the phrase "I *MUST* suffer" indicating certain events *must* take place to fulfill God's pre-determined fate for him.

His arrest *must* be one of those events, for without the arrest of Jesus there's no trial; without the trial there is no crucifixion; without the crucifixion there is no resurrection; and without the resurrection there is no Christianity. As we've demonstrated again and again, in chapter after chapter, the Gospel accounts are, *again*, not only inconsistent with one another, but they also present irreconcilable discrepancies.

THE LAST SUPPER

In Mark, we are told that the disciples ask Jesus, on the first day of the Feast of Unleavened Bread, where he would like them to begin preparations for the Passover. Jesus gives them the directions to a man they must meet in Jerusalem, who will lead them to a guest room in his house:

> *"He will show you a large upper room, furnished and ready. Make preparations for us there." (Mark 14:15 NIV)*

Later that evening, Jesus and his disciples feasted on the customary lamb. Then, with their bellies full and with a satisfied air filling the room, Jesus reclines back on his chair and makes a shocking announcement:

> *"I tell you the truth, one of you will betray me – one who is eating with me." (Mark 14:17 NIV)*

The disciples are stunned by this revelation. One or two of them protest their innocence, and others demand to know who among them is a traitor. Jesus offers a cryptic reply, *"The one who dips bread into the bowl with me"*. He then delivers a promise of vengeance as forewarning, again contradicting his supposed forgiving and compassionate persona:

> *"But woe to that man who betrays the Son of Man! It would be better for him if he had not been born." (Mark 14:21 NIV)*

As a matter of later relevance, you see here that Jesus and his disciples are enjoying their meal in the evening. This is now the day of the Passover. The Passover is the Jewish holiday that celebrates God's holocaust of all first-born boys in Egypt as a means to help his chosen people escape from that nation, documented in the Book of Exodus (but for which there is no supporting evidence for, despite the meticulous record keeping of the Egyptians).

We then come to the infamous denial of Peter. As the wine flowed, Jesus became increasingly accusatory, as often drunkards do. Eventually he turned his indignation towards Peter, reciting the prophecy of Zechariah 13:7:

"I will strike the shepherd and the sheep of the flock will be scattered." (Matthew 26:31 NIV)

Jesus, using this Old Testament prophecy, predicted that as a result of tough times ahead, his weakest followers would disperse into the night so as to save themselves. Naturally, Peter firmly denies this could ever be true and replies:

"Even if all fall away, I will not!" (Mark 14:29 NIV)

THE COCK CROWS

Jesus kept on the offensive however, and countered Peter's defense testimony:

"I tell you the truth, this very night, before the cock crows, you will disown me three times." (Matthew 26:34 NIV)

This is in contrast to Mark's account:

"Before the cock crows twice, you will deny me three times." (Mark 14:30 NIV)

One could argue that there is actually no logical difference between saying 'before the cock crows once or twice'. In this instance, however, there is, because the cock does actually crow twice, which makes Matthew's testimony invalid.

Naturally, the dinner ended on a somber note and Jesus led his disciples, later that same night, to a town called Gethsemane. Once there he displayed his concern that the end was near for him:

"My soul is overwhelmed with sorrow to the point of death. Stay here and keep watch with me." (Matthew 26:36 NIV)

However, his disciples were tired and were unable to stay awake in order to stay on guard from the enemies that Jesus believed were assembling against him. But how many times did Jesus find his disciples asleep?

Mark: Three times.

Matthew: Three times.

Luke: One time.

John: No mention of this.

THE ARREST

As dawn approached, his disciples remained asleep, only to be awoken by Jesus' sudden declaration:

> *"Look the hour is near and the Son of Man is betrayed into the hands of sinners. Rise, let us go! Here comes my betrayer." (Matthew 26:45-46 NIV)*

As Jesus continued speaking, the doors flung open and armed Roman soldiers and mercenaries sent by the chief priests, stormed the house where Jesus and eleven of his disciples had setup camp for the evening. The armed assailants were led by, as predicted by Jesus, Judas Iscariot. Judas had pre-arranged a signal with the would-be captors and foretold them:

> *"The one I kiss is the man: arrest him."*
> *(Matthew 26:48 NIV)*

According to Matthew only, Judas stepped towards Jesus and pronounced, *"Greetings Rabbi!"* before planting a kiss on Jesus' cheek. The now infamous 'Judas kiss'.

What does John say? Well, with far less dramatic effect, John makes no mention of a kiss, as he writes that Judas' part in this coup was only that of leading the arresting officials to the house. Once there, Judas merely *"stood amongst them"*. Luke writes that Jesus anticipates a kiss but no actual kiss is mentioned.

It is very unclear why the Gospels needed to include the story of a betrayal, other than so a few more prophecies could be fulfilled. The Pharisees, Jewish elders and Romans did not require such a betrayal, however, mainly because, given the charges, Jesus could have been arrested any number of times. Jesus' identity, at least according to the Gospels, was hardly a secret amongst the religious authorities of the time, so why, then, is the 'kiss' required?

Moreover, why vilify Judas? If Jesus had to die to fulfill his God sent responsibilities, then someone was required to play the part of betrayer and ensure that Jesus was arrested. In this sense, Judas played that role perfectly for his master and as such, it is a role that God ordained himself. So again, why was Judas being punished for the defining role that proved he divinity of Jesus (i.e. the resurrection)?

Further revealing to the Judas mystery - the discovery of the Gospel of Judas in an Egyptian cave in the 1970s. This Gospel begins with the words:

"The secret account of the revelation that Jesus spoke in conversation with Judas Iscariot during a week, three days before the celebrated Passover."

The latter stages of the text say, *"you will exceed all of them. For you will sacrifice the man that clothed me."* This suggests that Jesus let Judas in on his plan to have him arrested, and that he needed Judas to play the part of betrayer. Naturally, Christians take offence to this suggestion as it contradicts Mark's gospel that quotes Jesus as allegedly saying:

"For I must die, as the Scriptures declared long ago. But how terrible it will be for my betrayer. For better for him if had never been born." (14:20)

So, whom do we believe? Mark's gospel is no more credible than Judas', and Luke's is no more believable than Thomas'. Therefore, Christians are left ultimately with a need to cherry pick the bits and pieces that they like the most. With that said, at the end of the day it's all hearsay. All of it hearsay, that simply doesn't corroborate with any external (non-existent) or internal (completely contradictory) sources!

One of the more curious incidents that are alleged to have taken place during the arrest of Jesus is the revelation of his ideology regarding the use of swords and violence.

Matthew writes that one of Jesus' disciples withdrew his sword as the Jewish priests stepped forward to arrest

Jesus. The unnamed disciple strikes the ear of the servant to the high priest. Jesus, in an effort to quell any sudden explosion of violence, says to his disciples:

> *"Put your sword back in its place," Jesus said to him,*
> *"for all who draw the sword will die by the sword."*
> *(Matthew 26:52 NIV)*

If Jesus is so against sword use and violence then why did he give the following command to his disciples?

> *"If you don't have a sword, sell your cloak and buy one. It*
> *is written: 'And he was numbered with the transgressors';*
> *and I tell you that this must be fulfilled in me. Yes, what*
> *is written about me is reaching its fulfillment. The*
> *disciples said, "See, Lord, here are two swords." "That is*
> *enough," he replied. (Luke 22:36-38)*

Well, which Gospel is right? If both are, Jesus is a hypocrite. If Luke is wrong then we can dismiss his Gospel as unreliable. Maybe we need a third party mediator? Now let's see, are there any other passages within the New Testament that refer to the use of a 'sword'?

> *"Do not suppose that I have come to bring peace to the*
> *earth. I did not come to bring peace, but a sword."*
> *(Matthew 10:34 NIV)*

Shit! Now Matthew is contradicting himself with his earlier *"die by the sword"* remark. You should be able to now see the god-awful way with which the New Testament is hacked together, right?

PETER'S FIRST DENIAL

With Jesus led away by the Jewish priests to face trial, Peter is all-alone in a courtyard when he is approached by a servant girl. The girl enquires, *"You were also with that Nazarene, Jesus?"* Peter denies her allegation, *"I don't know or understand what you are talking about."* Then moments later, he runs his ass out of there. In this instance it's Mark, Luke, and John that are unison. Matthew, however, says that he denied being or knowing Jesus to *"them all"* which is ultimately counter-intuitive considering that the courtyard was empty.

PETER'S SECOND DENIAL

Mark says that the servant girl followed Peter out of the entrance until she found him just 'standing around'; she then says to a group of nearby strangers, *"this fellow is one of them"*. Peter denies it again. But what of Matthew, Luke, and John's respective accounts, who does Peter deny knowing Jesus to?

*Luke: A little later **someone else** saw him and said, "You're also one of them?" "**Man**, I am not!" Peter replied. (22:57-58)*

*Matthew: He went out to the gate, where **another girl** saw him and said to the people there, "This fellow was with Jesus of Nazareth." (26:71-72)*

*John: As Peter stood among a **group of servants and officials**, warming himself from the cold, he was asked, "You are not one of his disciples, are you?" (18:18-25)*

Even within this miniscule narrative of the New Testament, the inconsistencies leap out of the page.

PETER'S THIRD DENIAL

To whom did Peter deny Jesus on the third and final interrogation?

Matthew and Mark say that it was to a group of men. Luke claims that it was a single, unidentified man, and John says it was to a servant. It seems the stories don't even tie together at the top, unfortunately so for Christians.

Furthermore, how many times did the cock crow, as foretold by Jesus in the moments leading to his arrest?

Mark: "Immediately the cock crowed the second time." (14:72)

Matthew: "Immediately a cock crowed. (Once)" (26:74)

Luke and John make no mention of the cock. I will resist the opportunity to make the obvious joke, although I really don't want to . So. Very. Much.

THE DEATH OF JUDAS

According to Matthew, Judas was riddled with guilt and remorse for fingering (not double-entendre) Jesus. The forlorn Judas decided to return the thirty silver coins paid to him by the Priests, for his part in Jesus' arrest.

Matthew then once again makes a major historical blunder and writes that this event fulfilled the prophecy of Jeremiah:

> "They took the thirty silver coins, the price set on him by the people of Israel and they used them to buy the potter's field, as the Lord commanded." (Matthew 27:9-10)

Only one big problem, silver coins as currency had gone out of circulation at least three hundred years before the time of Jesus. In fact, minted coins bearing the insignia of the Roman Emperor of the time were used and would have been provided as payment. Weighted currencies such as silver were used at the time of Jeremiah, but Matthew's lack of investigative journalism skills illustrates the fictitious nature of this story yet again. The final act of Judas has him throwing a piece of rope over a tree and hanging himself.

But the book of Acts completely contradicts this suicide story, and shows God once again to be an unforgiving murderous thug. The passage reads:

> ."With the reward he got for his wickedness, Judas bought a field; there he fell headlong, his body burst open and all his intestines spilled out." (Acts 1:18 NIV)

Did he hang himself or did his abdomen spontaneously perforate and his intestines fly out after inexplicable and unprecedented 'Hand of God surgery'?

For me the bigger question is why then, if he was remorseful and repentant of his actions, as Matthew had illustrated, did God end his life in such a grotesquely violent manner? The early Christians were eager to characterize God as a more loving, forgiving father figure in the New Testament, but they really did a number on themselves with this example of conflicting narrative. This is sheer unforgiving brutality. Nothing less. And for a person who did nothing more than played the part he was pre-ordained to perform... so much for free will, right? So much for being rewarded for doing 'God's Work', eh?

THE LAST SUPPER - BEFORE OR AFTER PASSOVER?

"On the first day of the Feast of Unleavened Bread, when it was customary to sacrifice the Passover lamb, Jesus' disciples asked him, "Where do you want us to go and make preparations for you to eat the Passover?"
(Mark 14:12 NIV)

Matthew and Luke duplicate the words of Mark in their respective accounts. The important part of this passage, however, is the fact that the Feast of Unleavened Bread, and the slaughter of the sacrificial lamb, takes place the day prior to the Passover. So when did Jesus and his disciples dine together? The answer is in this passage:

"When evening came, Jesus arrived with the Twelve. While they were reclining at the table eating" (Mark 14:17-18)

Hence, the Last Supper would have been an evening meal, the same day, as the day prior to the Passover, right? Wrong! In Jewish Orthodoxy 2,000 years ago, which is still tradition today, they measure a new day beginning at sunset, and finishing at dusk. Therefore, the last supper, by means of being an evening meal, was actually the first day of the Passover.

What this means is that Jesus was arrested, tried, and executed on the same day, the day of the Passover. John, however, does not mention the last supper, as his account has Jesus dead by the time of the Passover meal. In fact, John tells us exactly when it was that Pilate sentenced Jesus:

"It was the Day of Preparation for the Passover;
and it was about noon." (John 19:14)

This is completely at odds with Mark's account as he has Jesus hanging out with his disciples that day, giving them instructions to prepare for the Passover, before dining with them later that evening. But John has Jesus on this same day standing trial before Pilate.

Bart D Ehrman points out that Christian apologetics have attempted to twist and contort this irreconcilable difference by the use of twisted facts:

"I do not think this is a difference that can be reconciled.
People over the years have tried, of course. Some have
pointed out that Mark also indicates that Jesus dies on a
day that is called "the Day of Preparation" (Mark 15:42).
That is absolutely true – but what these readers fail to
notice is that Mark tells us what he means by this phrase:
it is the Day of Preparation "for the Sabbath" (NOT the
Day of Preparation for the Passover). In other words, in
Mark, this is not the same day before the Passover meal
was eaten but the day before the Sabbath; it is called the
day of "preparation" because one had to prepare meals for
Saturday on Friday afternoon."

As an objective observer might point out, it looks like each successive Gospel was just trying to correct the obvious mistakes of the one preceding it in the timeline. The obvious problem with this, however, is that it created further chronological discrepancies.

The most logical conclusion to these verses is that, Jesus, knowing full well that he was going to be executed the following day, made a decision to do something impulsive. As such, he created a cover story, one in which he asked his followers to propagate. This left him free to do all of those things that he'd always wanted to do before he did. Having studied the life of Jesus so intently, this probably involved feasting on some live children and participating in a gay orgy.

CHAPTER TEN

The Gospels on Jesus' Trial

What Christians Know

Shortly after his arrest Jesus is brought before the *Sanhedrin*, Jewish court, to face the charge of 'blasphemy'. After various witnesses are brought forward, with conflicting eyewitness testimonies, the Court finds that they are unable to bring judgment against Jesus.

That is until the frustrated Jewish priests ask Jesus, "Are you the Son of God?" To which Jesus replies, *"I am; and you shall see the Son of Man sitting at the right hand of power, and coming with the clouds of heaven."* The Court erupts in disbelief; the priests are apparently aghast that he would say such a blasphemous remark. *"What further need do we have of witnesses? You have heard the blasphemy; how does it seem to you?"* He is summoned to death, but because the Court has no real power, and certainly not to enact a death sentence without Roman authorization, he is subsequently brought before the Roman Governor, Pontius Pilate.

The Joke

An 8 year old in Texas wrote this summary of Jesus' trial:

"But the Democrats and all those guys put Jesus on trial before Pontius the Pilot. Pilot didn't stick up for Jesus. He just washed his hands instead."

How The Gospels Lied

If you pick up your copy of the Bible and peruse Mark chapter fifteen, you can read aloud the events of Jesus' trial before the Roman Governor Pontius Pilate in less than a minute. It's a short, no nonsense, and fairly un-dramatic trial. Pilate asks Jesus if he is the *King of the Jews*, a title that would earn the charge of treason and therefore death. Jesus replies, *"Yes it is as you say."*

The Jewish priests then apparently accuse Jesus of a number of other trumped up charges, and Jesus doesn't respond to any of them. Pilate is amazed and confused as to why the defendant, Jesus, would elect not to offer even a single word in his own defense. Especially considering the man's life was in his hands.

Mark writes that it was customary for the Roman Governor, during the Festival of the Passover, to release a Jewish prisoner. Pilate steps out onto the balcony before the crowds, and offers, *"Do you want me to release for you the King of the Jews?"* The chief priests, however, had put the word out amongst the crowd to request for the release of man named Barabbas, instead. Pilate then asks, *"What shall I do, then, with the one you call the King of the Jews?"* The crowd shouted, *"Crucify him!"* Mark closes off his short account of the trial with the following:

> *"Wanting to satisfy the crowd, Pilate released Barabbas to them. He had Jesus flogged, and handed him over to be crucified." (Mark 15:15)*

Jesus was then sent away to be flogged, mocked and spat on, before being crucified – a punishment which was set aside for ONLY the most heinous of criminals... certainly not befitting the 'crimes' Jesus was accused of. Moreover, fifteen short verses are all Mark has to say about the most famous trial in history. Stunning brevity from the Gospel that preceded his Synoptic contemporaries.

Matthew, copying from Mark, writes almost an identical account, with the only subtle difference being that the former goes the extra stretch to vindicate the Romans of the charge of *Deicide*. Matthew would save that for the Jews. After the crowd has denied the release of Jesus, Pilate says:

> *"I am innocent of this man's blood. It is your*
> *responsibility." (Matthew 27: 24 NIV)*

This comes right before the verse that would eventually give birth to western anti-Semitism, and lay the roots for atrocities committed against Jews for the almost two thousand years to follow:

> *"All the people answered, "Let his blood be on us and on*
> *our children!" (Matthew 27:25 NIV)*

It's almost impossible to calculate how many Jewish people have been slaughtered throughout the ages because of this single sentence contained in the New Testament, that makes all Jews collectively guilty of *Decide*. Here, Matthew not only singles out the priests or elders involved in the conviction of Jesus, but for all Jewish generations to follow. In fact, it wasn't until 1965 that the Church under Pope Paul VI ended the charge of *Deicide* against the Jewish people:

> *"What was perpetrated against (the Lord) in His Passion*
> *cannot be imputed either to all the Jewish people of that*
> *time or the Jewish people of our time ... Accordingly, all*
> *must be careful that nothing is taught about this matter*
> *in preaching or in catechizing that fails to agree with the*
> *truth of the Gospel and the Spirit of Christ."*

Pope, John Paul II, said in 1986:

> *"No ancestral or collective blame can be imputed to the*
> *Jews as a people for what happened in Christ's Passion:*
> *not indiscriminately to the Jews of that time, nor to those*
> *who came afterwards, nor to those of today."*

Isn't it sickening that a Pope must give one of mankind's most belated apologies? It's quite fitting considering that it was the original Catholics who ensured that this verse was propagated. Ultimately, we have come to know this to be the modus operandi of the Vatican – deny responsibility until it's impossible to continue to do so, vis-à-vis child rape scandal, AIDS and condoms, and the execution of Galileo.

Nevertheless, the false charge of *Deicide* endures, particularly in Eastern Europe and Russia, where the Eastern Orthodox Church resides. The charge of *Deicide* was again spread by Catholic Poland, albeit with less vitriol than in the past. Moreover, the accusation remains even within Hollywood cinematic viewing.

Mel Gibson's *Passion of the Christ* portrays the Jews as responsible for demanding the arrest of Jesus and his ultimate death by crucifixion. The film makes no effort to conceal the theological claim that the Jews are responsible for the death of Jesus, and that the sins of the angry crowd before Pilate remain the sins of their descendents forever.

One scene in particular, in the movie, has members of the mob intone the curse from Matthew 27:25: *"Let his blood be upon us and our children forever."* But Gibson, mischievously, has the crowd shouting this in Aramaic with no English subtitles. Presumably, in a thinly veiled attempt to not upset his Jewish Hollywood peers.

Luke's account is similar to Mark's but with distinct theological differences. In Matthew, and Mark – Jesus' response to the charge of calling himself the King of the Jews is more or less, *"If you say so!"* But Luke's response is of far greater drama:

> *"If I tell you, you will not believe me, and if I asked you,*
> *you would not answer. But from now on, the Son of Man*
> *will be seated at the right hand of the mighty God."*
> *(Luke 22:67-69 NIV)*

Big difference, huh? Furthermore, Luke adds another dimension to the trial by introducing King Herod. Herod was the Jewish ruler over Jerusalem, and the son of Herod the Great - who according to Matthew, caused Jesus' family to flee to Egypt. Scholars believe Luke to be on the wrong side of historicity with his solo claim.

Robin Lane Fox, *The Unauthorized Version: Truth and Fiction in the Bible,* contends that the story was invented by Luke based on Psalm 2 of the Old Testament, in which the *"kings of the earth"* are described as opposing the Lord's *"anointed"*, and also served to show that the Jewish authorities failed to find grounds for convicting Jesus. Wells gives emphasis to this in his book:

> *"The Gospel accounts of Jesus' trial and crucifixion are also replete with significant historical difficulties. Luke's account of the trial is an obvious summary of Mark's. Mark's, in turn, is full of imaginary dialogue and scenes concocted by Christian writers who, believing in the Messianic mission of Jesus, invented trial scenes and dialogue in which the Jews condemned Jesus for his status as the Christ."*

Now let us wrap this up with John's trial narrative; a narrative that is unique to say the least. Mind you, we've already become accustomed with John's particular brand outrageousness and incredulity.

The stand out difference, most certainly, is the lengthy and friendly dialogue between Jesus and Pilate, as though they'd been best mates or childhood pals. In Mark and Matthew, Jesus utters only three words throughout the entire trial, *"You say so"*, whereas in John's, the two characters get extremely chatty with one another and if we didn't know the ultimate ending to the Jesus story, we could easily conclude that the pair had a blossoming bromance in the making. And legend has it that Jesus gave great *moustache rides.*

At first, Pilate attempts to dismiss the case against Jesus completely, he says to the priests, *"Take him yourselves and judge him by your own law"*. The priests reply that they have no right to execute anyone, and therefore require Roman approval. Tailing this sentence is John's comment:

> *"This happened so that the words Jesus had spoken indicating the kind of death he was going to die would be fulfilled." (John 18:32 NIV)*

Pilate leaves the priests and enters the room where the guards are holding Jesus, and asks him directly, *"Are you the King of the Jews?"* Jesus replied, *"Is that your own idea, or did others talk to you about me?"* Pilate asks the equivalent of, *"Do I look like a Jew to you, and does this look like the face that actually gives a shit?"* Pilate then asks Jesus, *"What have you done?"* Jesus replied:

> *"My kingdom is not of this world. If it were, my servants would fight to prevent my arrest by the Jews. But know my kingdom is from another place."* (John 18:36 NIV)

"You are a king then?" said Pilate. Jesus answered:

> *"You are right in saying I am a king. In fact, for this reason I was born, and for this I came into the world, to testify to the truth. Everyone on the side of truth listens to me."* (John 18:37 NIV)

Pilate replied, *"What is truth?"* before leaving the room to talk with the Jewish priests again. Pilate is frustrated (just like I am each time I meet a Christian apologist, who are always freaking truth relativists!); he finds no reason to condemn Jesus and can't believe the fuss the Jews are making over him. And he says as much, *"I find no basis for a charge against him."*

The Jews argue their case to Herod some more, before Pilate eventually throws his hands in the air, and says:

> *"But it is your custom for me to release to you one prisoner at the time of the Passover. Do you want me to release 'the king of the Jews'?"* (John 18:39 NIV)

Jesus' fate is sealed from then on. If we now review Mark, for example, against John's, the testimonies are distinctively different perspectives. In John's gospel, Pilate declares Jesus innocent on three separate occasions and therefore he believed he did not deserve to be executed, whereas in Mark's gospel, Pilate never declares Jesus innocent.

We should ask ourselves, why? Well, it is no secret to anyone that the author John, via his writings, was openly hostile towards the Jews and he makes no attempt to conceal as much in his gospel. John narrates a scene whereby Jesus is talking to some Jewish priests. They're ridiculing him for talking in nonsensical parables and Jesus replies:

> *"Why is my language not clear to you? Because you are unable to hear what I say. You belong to your father, the devil, and you want to carry out your father's desire. He was a murderer from the beginning, not holding to the truth, for there is no truth in him. When he lies, he speaks his native language, for he is a liar and the father of lies."* (John 8:42-44 NIV)

Effectively, Jesus is implying that all Jewish peoples are the children of the devil and with John's narration of the trial, the charge of deicide will stick to the Jewish people until well into the 20th century (the Vatican finally withdrew this charge, as detailed earlier, reluctantly, in 1965).

John's anti-Semitism and sheer nastiness towards the Jews has been well documented by more accomplished devotees of Biblical scholarship than myself; it is, therefore, no secret or false innuendo. John was determined to pin the execution of Jesus squarely upon the Jews. Moreover, if we refer to John 18:36 again:

> *"If it were [my kingdom], my servants would fight to prevent my arrest by the Jews".*

This is, quite tellingly, the Jew hating author's attempt to imply that Jesus is no longer a Jew. I guess, amusingly, this may be part of the reason why most American living rooms are adorned with a portrait of Jesus above the mantelpiece. In those illustrations, he is characterized as a tall, longhaired white boy from Nebraska, rather than the short, stumpy, hairy, brown skinned Palestinian he would have most likely been.

Christian apologists will offer all kinds of feeble denials when attempting to refute the anti-Semitism of John, but it is widely accepted by scholars and is clearly bloody evident throughout his writings. For example, in the Gospel of John, Jesus portrays Christians as the beneficiaries of all that is positive and good (light; truth; spirit and life). In contrast, the Jews belong to the realm of Satan; death; falsehood; flesh and darkness.

John's Gospel is obsessed with "the Jews". Thus, "Jew" or "the Jews" is mentioned more than 70 times, compared to only 5 times in Matthew; 6 times in Mark and 5 times in Luke. Moreover, more than half of John's seventy references are anti-Semitic. For example:

- The Jews are portrayed as the persecutors of Jesus. (5:16: "So, because Jesus was doing these things on the Sabbath, the Jews persecuted him.")
- The Jews disapprove of Jesus. (6:41: "At this the Jews began to grumble about him.")
- The Jews seek to murder Jesus. (7:10: "Now at the Feast the Jews were watching for him and asking, "Where is that man?")
- The Jews claim that Jesus is possessed by a demon. (8:52: "At this the Jews exclaimed, "Now we know that you are demon-possessed!")

Most significantly, John implicates the Jews for the conviction and execution of Jesus, and this is evident in the fact that he introduces two Jewish trials of Jesus, in contrast to the single trial in the Synoptic Gospels. Moreover, John portrays the Jews as the moving force behind the crucifixion:

"Am I a Jew?" Pilate replied. "It was your people and your chief priests who handed you over to me. What is it you have done?" (18:3)

John also portrays Pilate as an indecisive, bumbling leader who is ultimately manipulated by the wicked and conniving Jews. Therefore, making "the Jews" directly responsible for Jesus' crucifixion.

"Finally Pilate handed him over to them (Jews) to be crucified." (19:16)

The title of "Christ killers" had now been securely placed on the Jews, thanks to John. These writings would result in some of humanity's worst atrocities, the Nazi Holocaust being just one. In *'The Holocaust as Interruption"*, Dr. E. Florenza (Professor of New Testament Studies) and Dr. D. Tracy (Professor of Philosophical Theology) say that:

"Christian biblical theology must recognize that its articulation of anti-Judaism in the New Testament, generated the unspeakable sufferings of the Holocaust."

Finally, Rev. James Parkes writes, Anti-Semitism and the Foundations of Christianity":

"It is dishonest henceforth to refuse the face the fact that the basic root of modern anti-Semitism lies squarely in the Gospels and the rest of the New Testament."

The truth, however, is much simpler. If there was indeed a historical Jesus, and he was in fact crucified, then it was because he was an uppity schizophrenic who pissed off everyone he met, but who also had a series of extremely good spin-doctor publicists.

CHAPTER ELEVEN

The Gospels on Jesus' Crucifixion

What Christians Know

The Passion narrative is arguably the most near and dear to the collective 'hearts' of the Christian faithful. That said, the story is actually an amalgamation of all four respective gospel accounts. A collage of passages taken from each that more than likely depicts the images you have in your own mind if you were asked to tell the story, as you know it, without referencing the Holy Book.

The Joke

From Monty Python's *Life of Brian:*

Centurion: You know the penalty laid down by Roman law for harboring a known criminal?

Matthias: No.

Centurion: Crucifixion!

Matthias: Oh.

Centurion: Nasty, eh?

Matthias: Could be worse.

Centurion: What you mean "Could be worse"?

Matthias: Well, you could be stabbed.

Centurion: Stabbed? Crucifixion lasts hours. It's a slow, horrible death.

Matthias: Well, at least it gets you out in the open air.

Centurion: You're weird!

How The Gospels Lied

WHO CARRIED THE CROSS?

Pilate hands Jesus off to the Roman soldiers whereby he is mocked, kicked, and spat upon according to all but John, and we will come to his testimony in a moment. The soldiers place a scarlet robe on Jesus and then *"twist together a crown of thorns and set it on his head"*. They then give him a wooden staff and kneel before him in mock praise and laughter, *"Hail, king of the Jews!"* before he is led away to be crucified. But now we come to contradictory accounts of who carries the cross to the crucifixion grounds for Jesus. The Synoptic Gospels all say the same thing:

> *"As they were going out, they met a man from Cyrene, named Simon, and they (Romans) forced him to carry the cross." (Matthew 27:32 NIV)*

Whereas John writes, *"The Romans took charge of Jesus, who carried his own cross."*

In what we have covered up to this point of New Testament analysis, we can be certain in our judgment that John's gospel is completely contradictory to almost every single other account of Jesus' life. Whoever he was, we can be sure that he was a nasty, anti-Semite author with a desperate anxiety to prove his belief that Jesus was God, in the wake of Jesus' then (100 AD) proven false promise to return.

THE INSCRIPTION

Once at the killing grounds, just outside of the city, the soldiers laid Jesus on the cross. What was the inscription written above Jesus' head, on the crucifix?

Mark: "King of the Jews."

Matthew: "This is Jesus, king of the Jews."

Luke: "This is the king of the Jews."

John: "Jesus of Nazareth, king of the Jews."

You may again accuse me of being a tad nit-picky in jumping on these differences, but I vigorously defend that accusation. You may have had a point if we were talking about a conversation that took place and a third party was narrating it, but we're talking about a physical inscription, and the Gospels can't even agree on these few select words.

Jesus is then hoisted vertically already nailed to the timber; passer-bys and the robbers crucified on either side begin to mock and hurl insults at him, such as *"He saved others but he can't save himself. Let him come down from the cross then we will believe in him."* All of these taunts are somewhat uninventive and lack any form of comedic timing, for my liking anyway. I mean c'mon, with Jesus' arms outstretched on the cross, I would have asked, *"Jesus show me how much you love me"*, or *"You can turn water into wine, but how about turning this rain into not being crucified?"* These jokes doing anything for you? No. Ok, let's move forward.

THE TWO THIEVES

This is a further historical embarrassment for the writers of the Gospels, as it is common knowledge that the Romans did not crucify common criminals such as thieves. This brutally inhumane execution method was reserved only for acts of treason against the State or disobedient slaves. It appears John was aware of this, as he doesn't mention the two men as being thieves; this is obviously his attempt to correct the error of the Synoptic Gospels.

What is it that the alleged men say to Jesus shortly after He his hoisted onto the cross?

Mark: There is no conversation between Jesus and the thieves.

Matthew: The two thieves mock Jesus.

Luke: Jesus says to the men, "Today you will be with me in paradise."

John: There is no conversation.

WHO WATCHED OVER JESUS?

This another historical fallacy exposed. John writes that:

> *"Near the cross of Jesus stood his mother, his mother's sister, Mary the wife of Clopas, and Mary Magdalene. When Jesus saw his mother there, and the disciple whom he loved standing nearby, he said to his mother, "Dear woman, here is your son." (John 19:25-26 NIV)*

According to John, Jesus is near enough to have a conversation with his mother, but we know for certain that women were strictly forbidden to enter the crucifixion fields. Matthew and Mark appear to be aware of this Roman policy, however, as they comment that the woman watched on from "afar".

JESUS' LAST WORDS

At approximately 9pm, Jesus offered his last dying words before taking his final breath. His last words were, depending on which Gospel you are reading:

> *Matthew: "My God, my God, why have you forsaken me?" (Matthew was quoting from Psalm 22 of the Old Testament)*

> *Mark: "My God, my God, why have you forsaken me."*

> *Luke: "Into your arms I commit my spirit."*

> *John: "It is finished."*

Personally, I would have thought Jesus' last words, shortly after being nailed to the cross, would have been, "Jesus on a stick, this fucking hurts. Can't breathe. Goodbye!"

We will come to the irreconcilable theological differences of these words very soon (are you excited?), but for now we will continue with the narrative themes.

WHAT HAPPENED AT THE POINT OF DEATH?

Well, according to John, what immediately followed the time of death is the bodies had to be removed, as the following day was the Sabbath. As was the custom, the Jews had a pact with the Romans that no Jewish bodies were to be left out in the open on the holiest day of the week. Therefore, Jesus body was removed, but to ensure he was dead they pierced his side with a spear and a dancing alien came out and entertained the amassed crowds. No, not really, but it would have been a whole lot more exciting if one did!

Nonetheless, if it's excitement you want then you can't go past Matthew's stand alone narrative; As Jesus cried his final words, *"Father why have you forsaken me?"* an amazing chain of events were set in motion:

> *"At that moment the curtain of the temple was torn in two*
> *from top to bottom. The earth shook and the rocks split. The*
> *tombs broke open and the bodies of many holy people who*
> *had died were raised to life. They came out of the tombs,*
> *and after Jesus' resurrection they went into the holy city*
> *and appeared to many people." (Matthew 27:51-53 NIV)*

As a Christian, this is probably not what you are told about the Jesus story, but also as a Christian, it's in the infallible Bible, so it is what you must believe. At the moment of Christ's passing an earthquake struck Jerusalem, an earthquake not recorded anywhere in history (or through retrospective geological analysis), and that dead people walked out of their graves and reunited themselves with their long line of descendents. Yes, zombies!

The advent of resurrected people leaving their tombs is again, another miraculous event that is completely unsupported by historical account. One would think that such an utterly incredible and literally miraculous incidence would at least warrant a small headline in some scroll or papyrus, somewhere. Not even Matthew's fellow

Gospels seem too bothered to even comment on the sight of zombies returning for one last pint at their local nearby tavern... and brains; tasty, tasty brains!

THE TEMPLE CURTAIN

The Synoptic Gospels do agree on one occurrence shortly after the time of Jesus' death, however. Well almost, and honestly, isn't a lightly corroborated version of events what you should expect from a supposedly infallible holy book? Nonetheless, they all seem to agree that the curtain inside the Temple tore in half... and not because it was ancient and a wind was blowing, or the story was made up, skeptics, no, it was because God was pissed!

John draws a blank on this, however. But do the Synoptic Gospels remain harmonized on this event? Unsurprisingly, they are not. What a shame. Matthew says that the curtain is torn *after* Jesus' death. Mark, likewise, says it occurs after, but then Luke messes it up for everyone:

> *"It was now about the sixth hour, and darkness came over the whole land until the ninth hour, for the sun stopped shining. And the curtain of the temple was torn in two. Jesus called out with a loud voice, "Father, into your hands I commit my spirit." When he had said this, he breathed his last." (Luke 23:44-46 NIV)*

CLOSER EXAMINATION OF MARK VS LUKE

If not for the brilliant New Testament scholarly analysis of Bart D. Ehrman, I may have missed the philosophical and theological differences between Mark and Luke with respect to the portrayal of the J-Man's death. In my opinion there is no person more brilliantly adept with fitting all of the pieces of the jigsaw puzzle together when it comes to dissecting the Bible. I love you, Bart.

In Mark's gospel, we are left with Jesus as a somewhat of a dejected figure that suffers so much that in his darkest hour he believes that his God has forsaken him. In the events leading to his death, he is betrayed by his friend Judas; denied three times by one of his nearest and dearest, Peter; berated by the Jewish priests; and then condemned by Pilate. He is kicked, whipped, and mocked by the Roman soldiers; taunted by criminals on the cross; and during this whole ordeal he utters not a single word. At his trial he spoke only three words, *"You say so"*. And yet, as the shadow of death descends upon him he cries, *"Father why have you forsaken me?"* Ehrman rightfully comments on Mark's gospel, "Jesus dies, in agony unsure of the reason he must die." He's gone from a tough hero-like figure to a whining pussy in only a few bloody paragraphs… what a cop out!

If we compare this with Luke's portrayal, the gulf of ideology between them couldn't be greater. Jesus is led away for crucifixion, but is not mocked or beaten by the Roman guards. Jesus walks towards the killing fields sure of the reason for his death, as he says to a number of women he sees weeping for him:

> *"Daughters of Jerusalem, do not weep for me, but weep for yourselves and for your children." (Luke 23:28 NIV)*

By Luke's account, Jesus sounds like a real ladies man here, and these are most certainly the words of a man at peace with his fate. Shortly thereafter, the Roman's nail Jesus to the cross, and because he is such a big and tough macho man, doesn't scream in agony and instead says:

> *"Father, forgive them, for they don't know what they are doing." (Luke 23:34 NIV)*

In Luke, Jesus even has a dialogue with his fellow condemned, and reassures them that:

> *"Truly I tell you, today you will be with me in paradise." (Luke 23:43 NIV)*

As the inevitable death approaches, Jesus does not feel forsaken but welcomes the next step of the journey; *"Into your arms I commit my spirit."* As Ehrman comments again;

"In (Luke) Jesus is completely calm and in control of the situation; he know what is about to occur, and he knows it will happen afterward: he will wake up in God's paradise, and this criminal will be there with him."

Further complicating this narrative is Mark's, *"Father why have you forsaken me?"*, as the final words of Jesus, is contradictory to what Jesus had to say to his disciples at the Last Supper:

"Then he began to teach them that the Son of Man must undergo great suffering, and be rejected by the elders, the chief priests, and the scribes, and be killed, and after three days rise again" (Mark 8:31)

THE BIG QUESTION here is; why would he think God had forsaken him, most especially if he knew he had to suffer in such a manner in order to fulfill the purpose he was sent to fulfill?

Maybe he was just human and realized, as death approached, that his life had been wasted on such bullshit futility. Perhaps he recognized he had effectively been manipulated by his 'father' in order to inspire belief in his bullshit philosophy. Or, and perhaps more tellingly, as the adrenalin began to subside from his system, perhaps he finally realized that he was, in fact, a flaming big mouth and shouldn't have actively pissed off so many powerful people.

CHAPTER TWELVE

The Gospels on Jesus' Resurrection

What Christians Know

Jesus was taken down from the cross. His lifeless body wrapped in white linen. His tomb sealed with a boulder. Three days later the tombstone is rolled away and his body is gone.

The Joke

Jesus dies and ascends to Heaven. The first thing he does is look for his father, as he has never met the man before and is curious to see what he looks like, and whether or not he looked like his mother or father, etc.

He looks high and low but cannot find him. He asks St. Peter "Where is my father?" But St. Peter says he doesn't know. He asks the archangel Gabriel "Where is my father?" But Gabriel doesn't know either. He asks John the Baptist "Where is my father?" But John does not know.

So he wanders Heaven, impatiently searching. Suddenly he sees out of the mist an old man coming toward him. The man is very old, with white hair, stooped over a little. "Stop!" Jesus yells. "Who are you?"

"Oh, please help me, I am an old man in search of my son." Jesus is very curious. Could this be his father?

"Tell me of your son, old man."

"Oh, you would know him if you saw him. Holes in his hands where the nails used to be, he was nailed to a cross, you know..."

"Father!" Screams Jesus.

"Pinocchio!" yells the old man.

How The Gospels Lied

There is little doubt that the narrative of the resurrection highlights the contradictions between the four Gospels better than any other plot line from the New Testament. There are numerous events and occurrences that take place in these passages that are central, and so important to the message and theology of Christianity, but the Gospels have radically different accounts for what happened. Moreover, of all the events that transpire, the four Gospels only agree on two events:

1. That on the third day after Jesus' crucifixion and burial, Jesus' tomb is found empty.
2. Mary Magdalene is one of those that discover the empty tomb.

On just about every other component of the narrative, the Gospels disagree as to what transpired, and often irreconcilably so. This must trouble those with even the deepest sense of faith. Of greater concern though, is the fact that scholars agree the most reliable gospel to be Mark's, and his gospel does not include mention of the virgin birth nor the resurrection. The final words of Mark's gospel are:

> *"Trembling and bewildered, the women went out and fled from the tomb. They said nothing to anyone, because they were afraid." (Mark 16:8)*

If you were to have read Mark's account of Jesus' death in the first, second, third, or even fourth century then you would know only that Jesus was crucified, buried in a tomb, and three days later his body went missing. The end. This is pretty important because it is easy to conclude that some opportunistic scoundrel found a new tomb and raided it and couldn't get Jesus' wedding ring off, so the grave robber took the body! Too much CSI?

Matthew and Luke add the resurrection narrative years after Mark, and then later scribes added in the final twelve verses of Mark – so as not to leave a barn sized problematic hole in the story. The nice thing is the Bible doesn't even try to conceal this from us, as the following wording is written in between end of verse 8, and start of verse 9:

"The most reliable early manuscripts and other ancient witnesses do not have Mark 16:9-20."

These facts are so damaging to the Christian belief that Jesus was resurrected after death, notwithstanding the obvious natural laws such an event would supersede. If the most simple and glaring explanation is the most likely, then resurrection has been written off, or at least, not written in.

THE BURIAL

This is Mark's complete account of the burial:

"It was Preparation Day (that is, the day before the Sabbath). So as evening approached, Joseph of Arimathea, a prominent member of the Council, who was himself waiting for the kingdom of God, went boldly to Pilate and asked for Jesus' body. Pilate was surprised to hear that he was already dead. Summoning the centurion, he asked him if Jesus had already died. When he learned from the centurion that it was so, he gave the body to Joseph. So Joseph bought some linen cloth, took down the body, wrapped it in the linen, and placed it in a tomb cut out of rock. Then he rolled a stone against the entrance of the tomb. Mary Magdalene and Mary the mother of Joses saw where he was laid." (Mark 15:42-47 NIV)

Mark says quite clearly that it was Joseph of Arimathea, Mary Magdalene, and Mary the mother of Joses who visited the tomb. Not surprisingly, Mary Magdalene. Because let's be honest, they were doing the crazy monkey bedroom dance.

Matthew and Luke concur with Mark, but whom does John say buried Jesus?

"Joseph of Arimathea was accompanied by Nicodemus." (John 19:38-39 NIV)

WHO WENT BACK TO THE TOMB?

*Matthew: "After the Sabbath, at dawn on the first day of the week, **Mary Magdalene** and **the other Mary** went to look at the tomb." (28:1)*

*Mark: "When the Sabbath was over, Mary Magdalene, Mary the mother of James, **and Salome** bought spices so that they might go to anoint Jesus' body." (16:1)*

*Luke: "It was Mary Magdalene, **Joanna**, Mary the mother of James, **and the others**." (24:10)*

John: "Early on the first day of the week, while it was still dark, Mary Magdalene went to the tomb and saw that the stone had been removed from the entrance." (20:1)

THE ROLLING AWAY OF THE STONE

Had the stone already been rolled away when Jesus' posse turned up, or was it done so before their own eyes?

Mark: "But when they looked up, they saw that the stone, which was very large, had been rolled away." (16:4)

Matthew: "Mary Magdalene and the other Mary went to look at the tomb. There was a violent earthquake, for an angel of the Lord came down from heaven and, going to the tomb, rolled back the stone and sat on it." (28:1-2)

WHOM DID THEY SEE THERE?

This is yet another event illustrating yet another example disparity between all four Gospels. They display such a stark contradiction between one another, and rather than just quote the respective passages in question, I will use the script from one of my favorite religious cartoonists Russellsteapot.com:

Priest: "Thanks everyone for participating in this year's Easter Pageant. All right kids we need to rehearse the part where it's Easter morning and the first visitors arrive at Jesus' tomb. Now who's in this scene?"

Child 1: "I am! Matthew 28:2-5 says an angel came down from heaven to greet them."

Child 2: "No, it wasn't an angel! It was a 'Young man', Just look at Mark 16:5!"

Child 3: "Hello! Luke 24:4 says very clearly it was 'Two men'."

Child 4: "Well according to John 20:1-2 nobody was there."

Priest: "Children, the contradictions don't matter! What matters is that we unquestioningly accept the magic of the resurrection even within the face of such glaring contradictions within the story."

Child 4: "Father, that was the most wonderfully concise summary of Christianity I have ever heard."

Priest: "Thank you child. It is blind submission to authority that got me where I am today."

WHAT WERE THEY TOLD AND WHOM DID THEY TELL?

This narrative has some serious implications for the Christian message if we accept Mark's testimony, i.e. the one written closest to the time of Jesus, as true. Mark says that Mary Magdalene, Mary the mother of James, and Salome return the tomb to discover that the stone blocking the entrance has been rolled away. Out of sheer curiosity they walk into the tomb and are met by a *"young man dressed in a white robe"*. The unidentified stranger says to the women:

> *"Don't be alarmed, you are looking for Jesus the Nazarene, who was crucified. He has risen! He is not here. See the place where they laid him. But go, tell his disciples and Peter, 'He is going ahead of you into Galilee. There you will see him (Jesus) just as he promised you."*
> *(Mark 16:6-7 NIV)*

Their instructions were clear - tell the disciples that Jesus has risen from the dead, and that he will appear to them, in the form of a ghost in Galilee to speak to them. What do the women do next? Do they carry out this order?

"Trembling and bewildered, the women went out and fled from the tomb. They said nothing to anyone, because they were afraid." (Mark 16:8 NIV)

What? They said nothing, to no one, out of fear? How would the disciples then know to meet JC Ghostly in Galilee? The answer is obvious; they wouldn't.

Subsequently, that's the end of the story according to Mark. The events concerning the life and death of Jesus are officially over. Wait! There are another twelve verses in the Gospel of Mark! But with the inclusion of a footnote, in the New International Version Biblical text, that reads:

"The most reliable early manuscripts and other ancient witnesses do not have Mark 16:9-20."

In other words, or better, in Ehrman's words, "It appears that the final twelve verses of Mark's Gospel are not original to Mark's Gospel but were added by a scribe in a later generation."

A reading of *Matthew*, *Luke*, and *John* only serves to entrench us in more and more questions. Take *Matthew*, for example; it's the angel that tells the attending women to inform the disciples to meet Jesus' ghost in Galilee. In his account the women are not portrayed as *"trembling and bewildered"* but as *"filled with joy"*, and accordingly they follow the instructions given and head to inform the others. Jesus, what a balls-up!

JESUS' FIRST APPEARANCE

Who did Jesus first appear to after his resurrection?

*Mark: "He appeared first to **Mary Magdalene**." (16:9)*

*Matthew: "So **the women** hurried away from the tomb, suddenly Jesus met them. "Greetings" he said. (28:8-9)*

*Luke: "Jesus appeared to **two of the disciples** on the road to Emmaus." (24:13-15)*

*John: "Jesus appeared to **the women at the tomb**." (20:13-14)*

JESUS AFTER HIS RESURRECTION

Let's not forget the fact that we are talking about a dead man's ghost here. It would be fair to assume that his first actions after death would be proportionately profound and illuminating. Perhaps a monologue about what dying was like, or about the quality of the weed in the afterlife, maybe even an absolution of the 'sins' of the Jews and Pontius Pilate for their role in 'freeing him' from his 'earthly vessel'.

Are you ready for this? According to Matthew, his first order of business, post-death, is to allow Mary Magdalene and the 'other Mary' to "clasp his feet" in worship. How one can clasp the feet of an incorporeal spirit in a non-physical form is more than baffling. John writes more or less the same, but with a little more of the misogynistic diatribe that we've come to expect from his gospel. His twist, is that he forbids the women to touch is feet because he has not yet ascended to Heaven, despite the fact that he allows Thomas to do so, a few days later.

Mark, however, writes that Jesus' first interaction is his command to his disciples to preach the Gospel:

"Jesus appeared to the Eleven as they were eating; he rebuked them for their lack of faith and their stubborn refusal to believe those who had seen him after he had risen. He said to them, "Go into all the world and preach the good news to all creation." (Mark 16:14-15 NIV)

WHEN DID JESUS ASCEND TO HEAVEN?

Now that Jesus has risen from the dead and spoken with his disciples, he is ready to ascend into Pixie Land. So, when does he decide to climb the stairway to heaven?

Mark: Jesus ascends while he and his disciples are seated at a dinner table in Jerusalem. (14-19)

Matthew: Doesn't mention the ascension at all.

Luke: Jesus ascends after dinner in Bethany, on the same day as the resurrection. (24:50-51)

John: Doesn't mention the ascension.

Moreover, the Book of Acts, which is attributed to the same author as Luke (whose real identity is an absolute mystery), details Jesus' ascension into to Heaven as taking place at Mt. Olivet (Acts 1:9-12) some forty whole days after the resurrection. This obviously contradicts what the same lazy author wrote, as described above, in Luke 24:50.

The final words of the Gospels as presented by Mark:

"Then the disciples went out and preached everywhere, and the Lord worked with them and confirmed his word by the signs that accompanied it." (Mark 16:20 NIV)

CHAPTER THIRTEEN

The Gospels on
Why Jesus Had To Die

The variant views between Mark and Luke's reasoning as to why Jesus had to die is yet another scud-missile into the ship stern that is Christianity's credibility. Familiar with the fact Mark's Gospel preceded the other three, and as such, is potentially more credible than the others (Matthew and Luke) who subsequently used Mark as the source for their own.

Well, there is a passage found in Mark that is of extreme fundamental theological significance but is not found in Luke's. Therefore, it is safe to presume that Luke made a sole arbitrary decision to omit it.

The passage in question is:

"For even the Son of Man did not come to be served,
but to serve, and to give his life as a ransom for many."
(Mark 10:45 NIV)

It's Mark's view that Jesus' crucifixion and death was a pre-ordained human sacrifice to atone for the original sin, Adam's sin. In other words, his death was one of atonement.

The author of Luke writes in the Book of Acts, however:

"Therefore let all Israel be assured of this: God has made this Jesus, whom you crucified, both Lord and Christ."

When the people heard this, they were cut to the heart and said to Peter and the other apostles, "Brothers, what shall we do?"

Peter replied, "Repent and be baptized, every one of you, in the name of Jesus Christ for the forgiveness of your sins. And you will receive the gift of the Holy Spirit." (Acts 2:36-38 NIV)

Luke's view is believers will be rewarded for directly asking for the forgiveness of their own sins. In case you're thinking that this is just a game of literary semantics in play here, it's not. So there! These are fundamental differences; atonement and forgiveness is not the same thing. I will submit to Ehrman, to illustrate:

> "Suppose you owe me a hundred dollars but can't pay. There are a couple of ways the problem could be solved. Someone else (a friend, your brother, your parents) could pay the hundred dollars for you. That would be like atonement: someone else pays your penalty. Or, instead of that, I could simply say, "Never mind, I don't need the money." That would be like forgiveness, in which no one pays and God simply forgives the debt." (p 94)

Paul, while not one of the four Gospels, but whose writings predated Mark and Luke, writes:

> "For I handed on to you as of first importance what I in turn had received: the Christ died for our sins in accordance with the scriptures, and that he was buried, and that he was raised on the third day in accordance with the scriptures, and that he appeared to Cephas, then to the twelve. (Corinthians 15:3-5)

Thus supporting Mark's position that Jesus died to atone for 'our sins', ie original sin. Therefore, Luke is all out on his own – proving once again the Gospels are not in unison.

What I could never understand about Jesus' 'sacrifice' is that - if he were God, as John contends, then what kind of sacrifice was it? He was living in the first century Jerusalem, disease was rife, it was dusty and oppressively hot, everyone hated him, and his closest friends betrayed him. Heaven and Nirvana - were described by sages and prophets as *"paradise", that is, despite the dragons and creepy beasts detailed in Revelations.* As such, how can Jesus claim to be sacrificing when his death meant leaving the earthly shit-hole for the comfort of eternal life in a wondrous kingdom, where he'd truly be king? If this is the case, then what the hell was he waiting for? I'd have volunteered for a crucifixion well before age 33. "Hurry, here's a cross and some nails. Let's get this thing started." But that's me!

Colonel Robert Green Ingersoll, a Civil War veteran, political leader, and orator during the Golden Age of Free-Thought, suggests that the concept of Jesus' atonement is simply an extension of the Mosaic tradition. This is the tradition of blood sacrifice and is referred to by many as the "enemy of morality."

With all of the above said, however, we are left with a very interesting conundrum; if evolution is indeed the evidence based fact that it is, then Adam and Eve never existed and Jesus' death is, by reverse logic, made irrelevant.

For man living in the first to seventeenth centuries, evolution was neither documented, discovered, nor understood. Thus Jesus' atonement for the original sin is redundant. The sin committed by Adam and Eve, that of eating fruit from the Tree of Knowledge, an act that saw their immortality withdrawn and their expulsion from the Garden of Eden, never occurred. As such, what did Jesus die for, exactly?

I'm not here to convince you of the fact of evolution, far greater minds than I can do that easily in my stead. Before you read the following excerpt from esteemed evolutionary biologist, bestselling author and outspoken atheist, Professor Richard Dawkins' book, *The Greatest Show on Earth*, remember that simple little conundrum above. If Adam, Eve, the Garden of Eden, the Snake and the creator of heaven and earth never existed (i.e. as an extrapolation of biological evolution by way of natural selection) then what was the purpose of Jesus?

The answer is simple; there is none.

"Evolution is a fact. Beyond reasonable doubt, beyond serious doubt, beyond sane, informed, intelligent doubt, beyond doubt evolution is a fact. The evidence for evolution is at least as strong as the evidence for the Holocaust, even allowing for eye witnesses to the Holocaust. It is the plain truth that we are cousins of chimpanzees, somewhat more distant cousins of monkeys, more distant cousins still of aardvarks and manatees, yet more distant cousins of bananas and turnips ... continue the list as long as desired. That didn't have to be true. It is not self-evidently, tautologically, obviously true, and there was a time when most people, even educated people, thought it wasn't. It didn't have to be true, but it is. We know this because a rising flood of evidence supports it. Evolution is a fact, and [my] book will demonstrate it. No reputable scientist disputes it, and no unbiased reader will close the book doubting it."
(The Greatest Show on Earth, Richard Dawkins)

Theologically speaking, cannot call him or herself a Christian while maintaining belief in evolutionary science. The two are absolutely mutually exclusive.

CHAPTER FOURTEEN

Jesus According To Paul

The Conversion of Saul to Paul

Oh, how I love this guy so, Saint Paul. He was arguably the greatest marketer or publicist to ever grace the planet and most certainly the first tabloid journalist of the ancient world. How can you not love the creator of the West's most dominant religion? As we will soon discover, Christianity, the religion, has less to do with Jesus and much more to do with Paul. Although 'Paulinity' or the 'Pauline Christology' doesn't have the same 'ring' to it as Christianity, the theology is uniquely, incontrovertibly and unquestionably his.

Born with the name Saul, he claimed that he was Jew of the tribe of Benjamin, from a well-established Pharisee family in Tarsus, thus he was known as Saul of Tarsus. According to the Book of Acts, and although later contradicted by Paul himself, he studied in Jerusalem under the tutelage of the leader of the Pharisees, Gamaliel.

This account is, however, subject to reasonable doubt as the tribe of Benjamin had ceased to exist well before Saul/Paul came along. This contradiction is supported by the Ebionites, as they claimed he came from a family of newly converted Jews, with a background in the tent-making business.

The Bible first introduces us to Saul, prior to taking the name Paul (which he adopted post-conversion to Christianity), in the Book of Acts. His introduction is somewhat perplexing as he enters the scene completely without reference or context. It's as though he just wrote himself into the script without anyone noticing, and hoped that he'd just be accepted as part of the cast. Apparently, it worked:

> *"Meanwhile, Saul was still breathing out murderous threats against the Lord's disciples (Christians). He went to the high priest and asked him for letters to the synagogues in Damascus, so that if he found any [Christians] there who belonged to the Way, whether men or women, he might take them as prisoners to Jerusalem."*
> *(Acts 9:1-2 NIV)*

It's odd that the writer makes no previous reference to Saul; while at the same time introduces him in such an overt and apparently well established manner. Nonetheless, we are told that Saul hated Christians so much for their radical non-Jewish teachings and un-circumcised penises, that he loved nothing more than arresting and getting them stoned... sorry, stoning them. *"Hand carved rocks for 1 shekel a packet!"*

We are not told for what duration did Saul the 'Christian hunter' carry out his mercenary deeds but we are given an elaborate description of his miraculous conversion. For the Bible says:

> *"As he neared Damascus on his journey, suddenly a light from heaven flashed around him. He fell to the ground and heard a voice say to him, "Saul, Saul, why do you persecute me?"*

> *"Who are you, Lord?" Saul asked. "I am Jesus, whom you are persecuting," he replied. "Now get up and go into the city, and you will be told what you must do."*
> *(Acts 9:3-6 NIV)*

Paul was not traveling alone; he was with several buddies at the time that Jesus' ghost spoke to him on the road to Damascus. What is it that his fellow travelers heard?

> *Acts 9:7: "The men traveling with Saul stood there speechless; they heard the sound but did not see anyone."*

Acts 22:9: "My companions saw the light, and they understood ('akouo') *the voice of him who was speaking to me."

Acts 26:14: "We all fell to the ground, and I heard a voice saying to me in Aramaic, 'Saul, Saul, why do you persecute me? It is hard for you to kick against the goads."

All of the above passages are from the same author, Luke. But we are unable to reconcile whether or not Paul's companions "stood" or "fell", upon hearing the voice. Nor can we determine whether they knew it was Jesus ("Him") or did not. This is yet another example of the same author contradicting himself. Didn't they have editors back in those days?

This passage makes the Christian faith even less plausible though, if that were at all possible. Not only did Paul invent Christian theology, but he also did so without any conversation or meeting with the living Jesus, and, though this should hardly be surprising by this point, no eyewitness testimony.

Paul's only dialogue with the corner piece of his religion was a chat with the ghost of Jesus on the road to Damascus. The adage of, *'If you speak to God you're faithful, if God speaks to you then you are a lunatic'*, rings loudly for me at this point. Nonetheless, Paul picks himself up from the ground, dusts off his garment, and then comes to the sudden realization that he cannot see. His sight is lost, thus his servants lead him by hand into the city of Damascus.

---

* The differences in these three passages also illuminate a dishonest attempt by Bible translators to reconcile the variations of Luke's accounts. For example, Acts 22:9 in the New International, and the New American versions actually read as:

*"My companions saw the light, but **they did not understand** the voice of him who was speaking to me."*

However, the Greek word *"akouo"* is translated 373 times in the New Testament as *"heard"*. The only occasion where this translation does not apply is in Acts 22:9. Why? A sneaky effort to reconcile this conflicting passage in the hope you weren't paying attention. These guys were good!

Now safely at a friend's house within the city, Saul sits there in shock and does not sleep or eat for three days. All the while his sight was still lost.

What I find somewhat ridiculous though is that he claimed to have seen Jesus and this is why he went blind. But isn't that a contradiction in terms? How does one see something that is invisible? God, I love the Bible.

We now find ourselves at a contradictory crossing point between Paul's own account and that of the writer of the book of Acts. According to the writer known as Luke, Paul was led via a vision to a disciple by the name of Ananias, with specific instructions; *"Go to the house of Judas on Main Street and ask for a man named Saul from Tarsus, for he is praying. Once there lay your hands on him and his sight will be restored."*

Ananias tried to argue with God that he did not want to lay hands on a man who had persecuted Christian Jews so viciously and joyfully. God replies:

"This man is my chosen instrument to carry my name before the Gentiles and their kings and before the people of Israel. I will show him how much he must suffer for my name." (Acts 9:15-16 NIV)

Ananias carried out God's orders as instructed, laying his hands on Saul. As he did so, the 'fish-scales' covering Saul's eyes fell to the ground and he could see again.

Obviously grateful for his restored sight, Saul immediately began to preach the word of 'Jesus the Savior' in synagogues throughout Jerusalem and Damascus. The chief priests were mortified upon learning of his conversion and immediately concocted a plan to capture and kill him. Saul miraculously stumbled onto their plot and fled, and in the process changed his name to Paul. Henceforth, becoming the most important man in the marketing of brand Jesus.

This story is all fine and dandy until you read Paul's own testimony about what happened directly following his meeting with Jesus' ghost on the Damascus Highway. In his letter to Galatians, Paul writes:

*"But when God, who set me apart from birth and called me by his grace, was pleased to reveal his Son in me so that I might preach him among the Gentiles, **I did not consult any man,** nor did I go up to Jerusalem to see those who were apostles before I was, but I went immediately into Arabia and later returned to Damascus." (Galatians 1:17 NIV)*

This completely contradicts what the author known as Luke wrote in the Book of Acts. So, whom do we trust? Do we trust Luke when he says that Paul sought Ananias after meeting Jesus' ghost, or do we trust Paul 'himself'?

Choosing to believe the more probable account of Paul seems the most logical way to go. With that said, however, we have then, by process of elimination called Luke a liar. As such, how can we then trust anything that Luke had to say in his gospel that was not already previously written in Mark's?

Paul's conversion does pose a significant conundrum for Christianity; as it demonstrates that a miracle was required to convert Paul. If we are led to believe, as documented in Paul's letters, that entrance into the kingdom of heaven is dependent upon our belief that Jesus was the Son of God, and he died for our sins, then it's only fair that we ask; where is our personalized miracle to convert us?

I promise you this, if Jesus took the time to come down from cloud-land to convert me, I wouldn't remain an atheist for very long. I also guarantee that there'd be no other religions or apostates if Jesus would get off his lazy ass and appear to humanity. Given that Paul asserts that we are denied passage to heaven if we don't believe what was only revealed to him by way of miracle, then where the fuck is mine? Surely, it can't be too much to ask.

What makes Paul so special is that he takes sole ownership of the concocted ideology that Jesus' death was required to save mankind from sin. Rather than seeing Jesus as a Hebrew messiah, the like of Moses who was sent to bring the Jews out of bondage, Paul saw him as a salvation deity whose atoning death was required to pave the way for everlasting life in heaven.

It appears, however, that Paul was heavily influenced by the mythology of neighboring pagan nations who worshipped gods such as Attis, and Dionysus. These gods share an eerie symmetry and similarity with the story of Jesus:

- **Attis of Phyrigia**: Born of the virgin Nana on December 25th, crucified, placed in a tomb and after 3 days, was resurrected.
- **Dionysus of Greece**: Born of a virgin on December 25th, was a traveling teacher who performed miracles such as turning water into wine.

These are also gods that found divinity via a violent death. Religious mythology borrowing from neighboring religious mythology is how all religions came about; after all we are only talking about a geographical region that spanned the same distance as Los Angeles to Phoenix.

Paul writes in his letter to the church in Rome:

"We were therefore buried with him through baptism into death in order that, just as Christ was raised from the dead through the glory of the Father, we too may live a new life. If we have been united with him in his death, we will certainly be united with him in his resurrection. For we know that our old self was crucified with him so that the body of sin might be done away with, that we should no longer be slaves to sin – because anyone who has died has been freed from sin." (Romans 6:4-7 NIV)

For Paul the path to heaven is an easy one. This is what made Christianity so attractive to non-Jews, the Gentiles:

"That if you confess with your mouth, 'Jesus is Lord,' and believe in your heart that God raised him from the dead, you will be saved." (Romans 10:9 NIV)

Is it any wonder that Christianity took off so easily and pervasively in the ancient world as it has after the founding of the United States? Effectively, Paul made his new religion one that could be followed from the sofa, all you have to do is shout, *"Jesus is Lord"* and you're guaranteed immortal life in freaking paradise. Better yet, you don't need to sacrifice animals, attend weird ceremonies (except the whole transubstantiation cannibalism ritual) or be circumcised... and bacon wrapped in shellfish is back on the menu! Pure genius!

Lewis Black Waxes Lyrical Catholic Converting Jews

If you have read my first book, you will know that I am a shameless fan of comedian Lewis Black. In keeping with my one-sided bro-mance with Mr. Black, (please call me, Lewis) we can pause for a moment to read his take on Jews converting to Catholicism, the original Church:

"I have never understood converting from Judaism to Catholicism. Or, for that matter, converting the other way.

To begin with, both religions are squarely rooted in guilt. And while each faith deals with guilt very differently; neither does a good job of coping with it. So why switch from one to the other?

At least that's what I thought until I read about the French Cardinal Jean-Marie Lustiger, who passed away in 2007. Born a Jew in Paris in 1926, Lustiger was sent by his parents to Orleans to live with a Catholic woman after Paris fell to the Nazis at the beginning of World War II. At the age of thirteen – ironically, when he should have been bar mitzvahed – Lustiger decided to convert to Catholicism. His parents, to say the least, weren't pleased. Apparently, they did not see the humor in it.

After taking a degree as the Sorbonne, Lustiger studied for the priesthood and was ordained in 1954. He rose through the ranks of the Catholic Church and eventually became bishop of Orleans and, later, the archbishop of Paris. At one point he started to learn Hebrew and thought emigrating to Israel. He wasn't so much marching to the beat of a different drummer as marching to the beat of a drummer with two separate drum kits.

"I was born Jewish," he said once, "and so I remain, even if that is unacceptable to many. For me the vocation of Israel is bringing light to the Goyim (non-Jews). That is my hope, and I believe that Christianity is the means for achieving it."

This may have been the ultimate Underground Railroad approach. But you have got to admire the balls on this guy. He proclaimed his Jewishness until his death. Which didn't seem to bother the Catholics as much as it did the Jews, WHO NEVER GRASPED LUSTIGER'S IDEAS ABOUT KNOWING GOD. He was even considered as a possible successor to Pope John II.

Could you imagine that? A converted Jew becomes pope. Oh, the damage we could have done.

As it turns out, we didn't need to get one of ours into the Vatican's top spot to screw things up. The Catholic Church has been managing to do it very well all on its own.

The Start of His Missionary

Paul's missionary campaign began in Antioch. He journeyed to Cyprus, where he converted Sergius Paulus, the governor of the island. It was probably at this point that he changed his name from Saul to Paul, in honor esteemed convert. Paul traveled throughout Asia Minor where he spread the promise of Jesus' return, and the reward of eternal life, Paul returned to Antioch. Approximately fifteen years after his first missionary tour he hit the road again, this time his journey taking him as far as Corinth, Greece. A couple of years later he partook in a three-year stay in Ephesus and it were during these missionary periods that he wrote his Epistles.

When the Epistles, or letters, made their way back to the Jewish-Christian leaders in Jerusalem, the shit literally hit the fan. The Jewish Christians were horrified that Paul was telling non-Jews that they need not follow the Mosaic Law, as they believed him to be constructing a pagan like religion, which he indeed was. You can imagine their dismay when they read Paul's letter to the church in Galatia:

> *"All who rely on observing the law are under a curse, for it is written: "Cursed is everyone who does not continue to do everything written in the Book of the Law. Christ redeemed us from the curse of the law by becoming a curse for us, for it is written: "Cursed is everyone who is hung on a tree." (Galatians 3:10-13 NIV)*

Effectively, Paul is trying to convey the message to his fellow Jews that he believed it impossible for someone to continue to do everything written in Old Testament law. He believed it was an unattainable standard, because no one has the capacity to be completely obedient all the time. But isn't Paul's new religion much ado about Jesus? What was Jesus' view on the Law?

> *"Do not think that I have come to abolish the Law or the Prophets; I have not come to abolish them but to fulfill them. I tell you the truth, until heaven and earth disappear, not the smallest letter, not the least stroke of a pen, will by any means disappear from the Law until everything is accomplished. Anyone who breaks one of the least of these commandments and teaches others to do the same will be called least in the kingdom of heaven, but whoever practices and teaches these commands will be called great in the kingdom of heaven. For I tell you that unless your righteousness surpasses that of the Pharisees*

*and the teachers of the law, you will certainly not enter
the kingdom of heaven." (Matthew 5:17-20 NIV)*

GASP! A contradiction in the bible? Holy foreskins, Batman.

I am not sure how Jesus could be any more direct in expressing his feelings on the matter. If you don't follow the law even better than the Jewish priests, *"you will certainly not enter the kingdom of heaven"*.

I can't find a single verse or quote in the New Testament where Jesus says; "You guys can throw out the law after I'm dead, because it was all barbaric bullshit designed to keep Moses' tribe from shagging donkeys." Jesus says nothing of the sort. This is solely and wholly Paul's attempt to broaden his fledgling religion's sales appeal.

Anyway, Paul is summoned to Jerusalem to give a 'please explain'. During lengthy deliberations at the conference in the city, an agreement was reached which decreed that non-Jewish converts need not observe the law of the Torah... and millions of penises everywhere breathed a huge sigh of relief. But remember this as a wonderfully framed illustration of how 'human' the origins of Christianity were. Decisions made arbitrarily and by committee no less, which was in deep contrast to what apparently Jesus' opinion on the matter.

For the next few years the Jewish-Christian elders in Jerusalem were at peace with their missionary Paul and he continued to spread the word that non-Jews could convert without cutting off the tip of their wieners. Word, however, trickled back to the hierarchy that Paul was denouncing or ridiculing Moses and the law:

"They have been informed that you teach all the Jews who live among the Gentiles to turn away from Moses, telling them not to circumcise their children or live according to our customs." (Acts 21:21 NIV)

An irreconcilable rift had begun between Paul and Jewish Christianity. Paul was soon summoned back to Jerusalem

JESUS LIED – HE WAS ONLY HUMAN

for a second conference, but he concealed his views, and cleansed himself in the Temple. The following day, however, the city allegedly descended into chaos as word spread that Paul had been ridiculing the memory of Moses:

"Men of Israel, help us! This is the man who teaches all men everywhere against our people and our law and this place. And besides, he has brought Greeks into the temple area and defiled this holy place." (Acts 21:28 NIV)

Paul was promptly arrested but tried to plead his innocence by using the old 'God spoke to me' defense:

"When I returned to Jerusalem and was praying at the temple, I fell into a trance and saw the Lord speaking. 'Quick!' he said to me. 'Leave Jerusalem immediately, because they will not accept your testimony about me.'" (Acts 22:17-18 NIV)

The mob didn't buy it, and if not for the intervention of the Roman police he'd have been killed where he stood.

The Roman commandant Claudius Lysias decided to bring Paul before the Sanhedrin to investigate the cause of the disturbance. Paul appealed to the Pharisee majority to acquit him, claiming himself to be a Pharisee.

Paul, in a daring 'escape from Alcatraz' like rescue attempt was liberated by the Pharisees, from the high priest. The high priest, however, resenting this escape, appointed forty men to assassinate him. Learning of the plot, Paul again placed himself under the protection of the Romans, who transported him by armed guard from Jerusalem to Caesarea.

This seems to me to be an indication of Paul's distinct lack of faith, that he did not ask or trust Jesus to watch over his welfare. It is somewhat akin to the Cock-In-A-Frock Pope requiring a bulletproof vessel for whenever he steps out into the public domain.

Regardless, the High Priest Ananias was infuriated, no doubt because of Paul's eluding his police taskforce in Damascus, and laid a charge of anti-Roman activity against him. Paul appealed for a trial in Rome before Caesar, which was his right as a Roman citizen. The insinuations made in *Acts* is that the Jewish "elders" were also implicated in the charges against Paul is not historically supported, since these same elders had just acquitted him in his Sanhedrin trial.

What perplexes me is that Christian Jews were apparently able to practice their Courts in Jerusalem, when Jesus had, according to the Gospels, been charged and executed as a heretic revolutionary? Isn't this the equivalent of former Mayor Giuliani allowing Al-Qaeda to establish offices in New York in the days after 9/11? It's just absurd!

Paul was then sent to Rome, and it is here that our information ends. Legend speaks of his eventual martyrdom in Rome, which led to his canonization as Saint Paul.

The Mystery of Peter

A further blow to the credibility of the Gospels' accounts is the fact that Paul is silent on just about everything Matthew, Mark, Luke, and John had to say. Remembering that Paul wrote his Epistles prior to the Gospel of Mark being written; they suggest the events reported by the Gospels were largely unknown to Paul. This further suggests that they were fabricated.

A classic example of this is that Paul writes about the disciple Peter, i.e. the same Peter that denied Christ three times shortly after Jesus' arrest. Paul makes no mention of what is a central component to the arrest-trial-crucifixion story, and a story that would have certainly been Peter's signatory swan song.

Moreover, Paul had motive to make mention of Peter's treachery. Why? Because they hated one another! Peter and Paul were the apostolic odd couple, and the New Testament clearly shows the two were lifelong verbal sparring partners.

At the centre of their animosity towards one another were their respective opposing views on whether non-Jews should be included in the early Christian Church. Peter was absolutely certain that the "unclean" Gentiles should be prohibited from gaining membership to Club Jesus, whereas Paul took his message mostly to non-Jews.

Now, if the Gospels were correct in their later written vilification of Peter, you would imagine then this would have been Paul's ace card, and one that he would have played to silence Peter's anti-Gentile views i.e. "Gather around everyone. Who are you going to listen to? Are you going to listen to me, or are you going to take the word of this treacherous snake that denied Jesus three times to save his own skin?" Checkmate! But, Paul is completely, totally and utterly silent on this event, and more to the point Paul never mentions a single event that Peter would have witnessed of Jesus, as his disciple. Therefore, another piece of the Jesus myth is debunked. Bam!

Paul's Knowledge of Jesus

It is staggering that Paul seems blissfully unaware of not only most of the events of Jesus' life, but also of all Jesus' teachings. Paul makes similar proclamations to the ones that Jesus made; for example, "love your neighbor as thy self"; "love your enemy"; "pay your taxes"; but he never once appeals to Jesus' authority. He never once says, "Blah, blah, blah, as said our Lord Jesus."

Paul urges his followers to adhere to Roman law, and to respect the Roman governors, which is odd since it was a Roman Governor, Pilate, who, according to the Gospels, ordered Jesus' execution. Is Paul unaware that Pilate played such a role? If he were, then why did he not mention it?

Put it this way; if Paul were our only source, our only document concerning Jesus, we'd know only the following: that he was a Jewish male; he went through some kind of out of body, after death experience; and that, in at least Paul's mind, Jesus would return to earth to punish the evil-doers (non-believers) and reward the righteous (believers). We would not know that he was born of a virgin; that he came from Galilee; was baptized; taught in parables; performed various benign and arbitrary miracles; and got all pissy at money changers and overturned their tables. Certainly makes you wonder how much Paul actually knew about Jesus? Also makes you wonder just how much of the Gospel accounts, considering Paul is the only biblical author who may have lived during Jesus' time, was embellishment or perhaps more aptly, bullshit. Well, let's see:

JOHN THE BAPTIST

The baptism of Jesus is a central component of the Jesus' story. It not only signified the commencement of his ministry but also gave confirmation that he was, according to the Gospels, the Son of God, and the Messiah. John the Baptist is a man awarded great importance by Jesus because he shared his penchant for apocalyptic prophecy. They both claimed that the world was coming to an end, and the righteous would be rewarded in heaven.

Furthermore, it was John the Baptist who gave the message of impending doom prior to Jesus saying the same, as the former said before Jesus' baptism, *"Even now the axe is lying at the root of the trees; every tree therefore that does not bear good fruit is cut down and thrown into the fire."* In this instance, the trees are metaphors for humans, and 'even now' means that the rapture was imminent.

According to the Gospels, Jesus placed an enormous importance on John the Baptist as a player in the apocalyptic prophecy. So much so, that when John the

Baptist was arrested, he and Jesus communicated while the former was in prison. As we discussed earlier in the book, John the Baptist sent a letter asking if Jesus were truly 'the' one:

"Are you the one who was to come, or should we expect someone else?" (Luke 7:20 NIV)

John the Baptist also believed Judgment Day was only a matter of months, or a few years away, and therefore this was he asking Jesus for a signal that 'the' time had come. Jesus replied by the disciple telegram network:

"Go back and report to John what you have seen and heard: The blind receive sight, the lame walk, those who have leprosy are cursed, the deaf hear, the dead are raised, and the good news is preached to the poor. Blessed is the man who does not fall away on account of me." (Luke 7:22-23 NIV)

This is Jesus sending a clear message that the things required of him to do prior to the apocalypse have been done, so brace for impact! Moreover, Jesus follows these words with an exaltation of John the Baptist:

"Yes I tell you, he is more than a prophet. This is the one about whom it is written: "I will send my messenger ahead of you, who will prepare your way before you." (Luke 7:26-27 NIV)

I think we have adequately proved just how important John the Baptist is to the complete narrative of Jesus, at least in the mind of the Gospels. But, what does Paul have to say about this key figure?

Paul never so much as even alludes to the traditions concerning John the Baptist. Paul is completely ignorant that such a man ever existed; let alone his ambivalence towards the significance to Jesus. Don't forget that it was John's arrest that kick-started much of Jesus' own public activity. Simply, one cannot dismiss the absence of John the Baptist from Paul's writings as merely an argument from silence. Remember the 9/11 analogy we used for the silence on the virgin birth? Well, same goes here.

THE BEATITUDES

One or two of Paul's epistles indicate that at least Paul was familiar with the expression the "good news" (evangelion), but the expression functions in a completely different manner as to that used by Jesus. "Blessed are the meek"; "for it is easier for a camel to walk through the eye of a needle than for a rich man to enter the kingdom of heaven"; are nothing like the parables and aphorisms that Paul presents in his letters. The "good news" for Paul is focused on what God did through Jesus on the cross, and what his death means in terms of his second coming and judgment.

JESUS' DISCIPLES

Paul makes one or two 'loose' references to a group of close followers of Jesus, as evident in his letter to Galatians:

"James, Peter and John, those reputed to be pillars, gave me and Barnabas the right hand of fellowship when they recognized the grace given to me. They agreed that we should go to the Gentiles, and they to the Jews." (2:9)

Alright, so he can name three of the twelve disciples and, admittedly, He makes mention in 1 Corinthians that Jesus appeared to the "twelve" shortly after Jesus resurrection, but what importance or relevance does Paul give to the "twelve", falling short of calling them "disciples":

"And from those who were reputed to be something (what they were makes no difference to me; God shows no partiality) – those, I say, who were of repute added nothing to me; but on the contrary those who were reputed to be pillars, gave to me and Barnabas the right hand of fellowship, that we should go to the Gentiles and they to the circumcised; only they would have us

186

remember the poor, which very thing I was eager to do."
(Gal 2: 6–10 NIV)

It is doubtful that Paul could have used more damning words for dismissing the disciple's relevance. His contempt is not only reserved for the "twelve" but also for the women in Jesus' life. There is no mention of Mary Magdalene, and nothing regarding Mary, the mother of Jesus. I am sure this fact sends chills down every good Catholic's spine. That said, we shouldn't be surprised by Paul's indifference of women, as this is the same guy that wrote:

> *"As in all the congregations of the saints, women should remain silent in the churches. They are not allowed to speak, but must be in submission, as the Law says. If they want to enquire about something, they should ask their own husbands at home; for it is disgraceful for a woman to speak in the Church." (1 Corinthians 14:33-35 NIV)*

JESUS AS A TEACHER

The Gospels distinctly describe Jesus as a teacher, with God having given authority, whereas Paul hardly makes mention of the 'living' Jesus being an authoritative source of instruction. Sixteen of the twenty-seven books of the New Testament are attributed to Paul, but on only three occasions does Paul invoke the title "the Lord". Rather, Paul proclaims Christ, dead Jesus, as a divine authoritative figure.

PARABLES

Paul is silent on Jesus' distinctive methodology for teaching the "good news".

CLEAN & UNCLEAN

The purity laws constituted one of the few points where Jesus pushed back against the Jewish tradition:

> *"Again Jesus called the crowd to him and said, "Listen to me, everyone, and understand this. Nothing outside a*

> *man can make him 'unclean' by going into him. Rather, it*
> *is what comes out of a man that makes him 'unclean.' "*
> *(Mark 7:14-16 NIV)*

If we read Paul's epistles to the church in Corinth and Rome we find that Paul had a certain degree of ambivalence on the subject of dietary laws:

> *"Do not destroy the work of God for the sake of food. All*
> *food is clean, but it is wrong for a man to eat anything*
> *that causes someone else to stumble." (Romans 14:20)*

> *"But food does not bring us near to God; we are*
> *no worse if we do not eat, and no better if we do."*
> *(1 Corinthians 8:8 NIV)*

What is surprising is that the issue of clean and unclean foods was a major dispute within the early churches throughout the lands of the Gentiles. In fact, confusion amongst early Christians regarding food was just as divisive a topic as circumcision, and we can see that in Paul's plea to the Roman Church, "Do not destroy the work of God for the sake of food". Why did Paul not call on Jesus' authority on the issue by citing what was written in Mark's Gospel, "Nothing can make a man unclean"?

This is further evidence that Paul was unfamiliar with anything Jesus actually said, and possibly my gay friend is correct in citing Jesus' *"Nothing outside a man can make him unclean by going into him"* as an endorsement of man on man lovin'.

Jesus' Miracles

The Synoptic Gospels describe Jesus as a reluctant miracle worker, while John proclaims Jesus' miracles as signs of his divinity. Where does Paul stand on the issue at hand? Paul again is completely silent, or worst, seemingly oblivious of a single miracle or sign that Jesus ever reputedly performed. The only time Paul refers to miracles is in Romans 15:19, but this is a reference to his own ministry, rather than anything Jesus did.

> *"I will not venture to speak of anything except what Christ has accomplished through me in leading the Gentiles to obey God by what I have said and done – by the power of signs and wonders, through the power of the Spirit of God. So from Jerusalem all the way around to Illyricum, I have fully proclaimed the gospel of Christ."*

JESUS IN JERUSALEM

The Gospels tell of Jesus' struggles with the Jewish authorities, and nothing exemplifies this better than the childish tantrum Jesus threw inside the Temple:

> *"On reaching Jerusalem, Jesus entered the temple area and began driving out those who were buying and selling there. He overturned the tables of the moneychangers and the benches of those selling doves, and would not allow anyone to carry merchandise through the temple courts. And as he taught them, he said, "Is it not written: "*
> *'My house will be called a house of prayer for all nations'? But you have made it 'a den of robbers.'"*
> *(Mark 11:15-17 NIV)*

We can presume that if Jesus had have only listened to Paul's teachings then Jesus wouldn't have been crucified, but then we'd have no resurrection, and then, of course, we'd have no Christianity. Paul writes in Romans:

> *"Everyone must submit himself to the governing authorities, for there is no authority except that which God has established. The authorities that exist have been established by God. Consequently, he who rebels against the authority is rebelling against what God has instituted, and those who do so will bring judgment on themselves. For rulers hold no terror for those who do right, but for those who do wrong. Do you want to be free from fear of the one in authority? Then do what is right and he will commend you. (Romans 13:1-3 NIV)*

THE PASSION

The death and resurrection is the most important, some may argue only important, aspect of Jesus' biography in the mind of Paul. After all, it was Paul that opined that without the resurrection there is no religion:

> "And if Christ has not been raised, our preaching is
> useless and so is your faith." (1 Corinthians 15:14 NIV)

What is bewildering is the fact that he provides so little detail on or about the Passion narrative... it's as though he had no idea that such events ever took place. Paul mentions that Jesus was arrested and crucified but that's about it; there is no mention of the 'empty tomb', for example. Moreover, Paul's account of Jesus' resurrection lacks any narrative or mythological elements typical of the Gospels. Paul writes only this of the resurrection:

> "So will it be with the resurrection of the dead. The body
> that is sown is perishable, it is raised imperishable; it is
> sown in dishonor, it is raised in glory; it is sown in
> weakness, it is raised in power; it is sown a natural body,
> it is raised a spiritual body.   If there is a natural body,
> there is also a spiritual body. So it is written: "The first
> man Adam became a living being"; the last Adam, a life-
> giving spirit." (1 Corinthians 15:45 NIV)

What do the nine aforementioned points tell us? They tell us we can learn nothing about Jesus from the teachings of Paul! This also confirms the scholarly consensus that Paul made little use of Jesus' life in his writings. Why not? We don't know, but it would appear safe to presume that the Gospels, as we had feared, fictionalized their respective biographies of Jesus well after the writings of Paul.

How can we make such an extrapolation? Because it is bleeding obvious that Paul had no idea about the myriad quests, the myriad magic and the myriad supernatural shit that the Gospels claim Jesus to have plopped out during his ministries.

But why then, is this discovery so pivotal to the Gospels validity? Simple, and in case you weren't paying attention; Paul's writings came first, literally a lifetime before the Gospels authors opined their respective works.

Nietzsche Has The Last Word on Paul

In 1888 the great atheist philosopher who coined the phrase, 'God is Dead', whose book *The Antichrist* centered on the teachings of Paul that contradicted Jesus':

> *"Paul is the incarnation of a type which is the reverse of that of the Savior; he is the genius in hatred, in the standpoint of hatred, and in the relentless logic of hatred…What he wanted was power; with St. Paul the priest again aspired to power, - he could make use only of concepts, doctrines, symbols with which masses may be tyrannized over, and with which herds are formed."*

So, I think, after this chapter, we can make four major conclusions:

1. Since Paul was alive and wrote his epistles well before the Gospels (Paul may possibly have also been lived during the same time as Jesus) and makes no mention of the vast majority of supernatural claims made in the Gospels; then the Gospels are BOGUS!

2. Since Paul makes no mention of the Gospel's (Matthew & Luke) claim that Jesus was born of a virgin who was directly impregnated by God; then this story is BOGUS!

3. Since Paul only talked to Jesus in visions (and there is no testimony to corroborate his claims) it is highly likely, if not a given, that he was suffering from delusional psychosis. It is only because he is attached to a story where one has already had to accept that the supernatural is real that one would accept his testimony. Consider that if we were to meet Paul today, it is highly likely, no, it is

bleeding obvious, we would have him committed to a mental institution... or placed him in the White House and called him a Bush.

4. Paul *is* the be all and end all of Christianity. The fact that I am writing this book is a testament to Paul's work, not Jesus'. And because of Paul's lack of detail or apparent knowledge of Jesus' life and times and ministry and miracles, there is now serious doubt as to whether Jesus ever lived at all!

CHAPTER FIFTEEN

Jesus, The Gospels & Paul on The Afterlife

The over arching objective of any religion, new or old, is to grow and prosper. In other words, you need a constant and ready supply of fresh, brain-dead recruits to empty their pockets into the pretty purple velvet tithing baskets. Paul was clever enough to latch onto Jesus' rapture prophecy and thus make the promise of heaven - central to his marketing strategy, and the Church has duly played its part in this in the centuries following this. This promise of the afterlife is what set Christianity apart from not only Judaism, but also other pagan religions in the fourth century that were flourishing under their own steam in these same regions.

Judaism, amongst others, invented sin. Until Moses told his Israelites that working or playing on the Sabbath was a sin on the footsteps of Mt Sinai, working or playing on the Sabbath was honky dory. Paul then tells his founding Christian members that believing Jesus died for their sins, having adopted the ancient ritual of 'scapegoating', will provide them passage to an eternal afterlife, fitted with mansions, 24/7 harp music and an endless supply of milk and honey. Too bad if you're lactose intolerant! Anyway, there's the sales hook for converting to Christianity, the promise you will live forever in paradise.

What about the downside for non-believers or unrepentant sinners? The unquenchable lakes of fire and brimstone of hell await, dear friend.

It is the doctrine of eternal damnation that provokes most of my ire towards the Gospel accounts of Jesus Christ. As we covered in chapter one, human suffering ended at the point of death... or at least that is what the Old Testament had to say on the matter. The unfortunate, the downtrodden, the huddled masses yearning to breath free could at least take comfort in the knowledge that their miserable earthly existence would eventually die... and be dead.

But then, along comes this big talking, grand promising Jesus, with his meek n' mild gumption, who effectively says, *"Death is just the commencement of true suffering should you not heed the bullshit frothing forth from my face."* In my opinion, there is no greater evil than this.

This evil surpasses any evil any human could possibly inflict upon another. An eternity of suffering is irreconcilable with any assertion that God, or Jesus, are the embodiments of love, compassion, and forgiveness. As Robert Ingersoll wrote:

> *"The myth of hell represents all the meanness, all the revenge, all the selfishness, all the cruelty, all the hatred, all the infamy of which the heart of man is capable."*

What Ingersoll was saying is that we created God in our image, and not the other way around. It's a product created in the deepest, darkest and most vile pits of humanity's imagination. With that said, it is most certainly a device of fiction; its sole purpose, to manipulate minds and behavior.

Albert Einstein famously opined the following in a 1955 New York Times article:

> *"I cannot imagine a God who rewards and punishes the objects of his creation, whose purposes are modeled after our own – a God, in short, who is but a reflection of the human family. Neither can I believe that the individual survives the death of his body, although feeble souls harbor such thoughts through fear or ridiculous egotisms."*

Does finite action or sin deserve infinite punishment? No, obviously not, and only a heinously wicked doctrine would suggest as much. This alone should be adequate to dismiss Jesus as a promoter of the dark, certainly not the light.

Hell is a destination fashioned in the depths of Jesus' own depraved thinking, and I truly don't know how to conceal my disgust for this utterly repugnant belief. It is a doctrine that is routinely thrust upon children at a very young age, *"If you don't please Jesus, you will burn in hell forever, but remember he does love you."* Ant this continuous fear mongering perpetrated against the children of every generation has left its mark. According to a 1990 Gallup Poll, more than 60% of Americans believe that there really is such a celestial city.

The brilliantly funny George Carlin one said on stage:

> *"When it comes to bullshit, big-time, major league bullshit, you have to stand in awe of the all-time champion of false promises and exaggerated claims, religion. No contest. No contest. Religion. Religion easily has the greatest bullshit story ever told. Think about it. Religion has actually convinced people that there's an invisible man living in the sky who watches everything you do, every minute of every day. And the invisible man has a special list of ten things he does not want you to do. And if you do any of these ten things, he has a special place, full of fire and smoke and burning and torture and anguish, where he will send you to live and suffer and burn and choke and scream and cry forever and ever 'til the end of time! But He loves you."*

Carlin perfectly surmised my thoughts on hell. Speaking of eternity though, you can see that we could spend eternity disgusting the hidden immorality and abhorrence of Jesus' teaching, but let's take a closer look to see exactly who says what about 'hell' in the New Testament.

By my count there are 162 allusions to Hell throughout the twenty-seven books of the New Testament, for which

70 are attributed to Jesus directly. One could argue that Jesus spoke about Hell more than another topic based on his recorded teachings.

Hell itself, as in the word "Hell", is mentioned twenty-four times:

Matthew: 12 times.

Mark: 3 times.

Luke: 5 times (including Acts).

John: 0.

Revelations: 4 times (which is attributed to the authorship of John).

Paul doesn't mention Hell, or even the concept of eternal damnation at all; not once! But we will come to him in a moment. First, let's look at what the Gospels recorded Jesus as having said on the matter.

John the Baptist was the first character of the New Testament to speak of Hell, and it's his use of the phrase "unquenchable fire" that grabs the attention:

> "I baptize you with water for repentance. But after me will come one who is more powerful than I, whose sandals I am not fit to carry. He will baptize you with the Holy Spirit and with fire. His winnowing fork is in his hand, and he will clear his threshing floor, gathering his wheat into the barn and burning up the chaff with unquenchable fire." (Matthew 3:11-12 NIV)

John the Baptist is speaking to his gathered followers when he warns them of the arrival of the true 'superstar', who will work on behalf of God and separate the righteous from the sinners - the latter being thrown into everlasting fire. John the Baptist has opened the doorway to Hell, and Jesus gladly accepts the invitation. The following passage is the first time Jesus mentions Hell:

> "You have heard that it was said to the people long ago, 'Do not murder, and anyone who murders will be subject to judgment.' But I tell you that anyone who is angry

> *with his brother¹ will be subject to judgment. Again,*
> *anyone who says to his brother, 'Raca' is answerable to*
> *the Sanhedrin. But anyone who says, 'You fool!' will be in*
> *danger of the fire of hell." (Matthew 5:21-22 NIV)*

Jesus uses better imagery than that in latter passages though, as evident:

> *"So shall it be at the end of the world: the angels shall*
> *come forth, and sever the wicked from among the just, and*
> *shall cast them into the furnace of fire: there shall be*
> *wailing and gnashing of teeth" (Matthew 13:49-50).*

Paul on Hell

As mentioned earlier in this chapter, there are well over a hundred passages from scripture that reference the 'Devil's lair' and most are attributed directly to Jesus. What is interesting about this is that Paul has an opposing view. Central to his ministry was the second coming and the end of times - whereby the righteous will ascend to heaven alongside Jesus - but he never exclaimed that sinners, doubters, evildoers, or George Bush, would be sent down stairs to play 'hide the pineapple in your anus' with Satan. It was Paul's view that not ascending to Heaven to hang out with God and Jesus, and many large-breasted blonde women, was punishment enough. Paul simply puts it:

> *"They will be punished with everlasting destruction and*
> *shut out from the presence of the Lord and from the*
> *majesty of his power." (2 Thessalonians 1:9 NIV)*

This is more in line with an Old Testament view that death is the final everlasting destruction. The end. Game over. There is no eternal torture form Paul's standpoint, there is simply nothing.

Who are we to believe? The Gospels alleged accounts of Jesus, or Paul?

Answering the above question aside, it still doesn't get us out of interpretative purgatory because the Book of Revelation - attributed to the same author of the Gospel of John - decrees that only 144,000 Jewish men will enter the kingdom of Heaven, and thus enjoy an eternal life. Too bad for everyone outside of this select little group, and too bad for all non-Jews, which makes a mockery of Paul's preaching to the Gentiles:

> *"Then I looked, and there before me was the Lamb,*
> *standing on Mount Zion, and with him 144,000 who had*
> *his name and his Father's name written on their*
> *foreheads. And I heard a sound from heaven like the roar*
> *of rushing waters and like a loud peal of thunder. The*
> *sound I heard was like that of harpists playing their harps.*
> *And they sang a new song before the throne and before the*
> *four living creatures and the elders. No one could learn*
> *the song except the 144,000 who had been redeemed from*
> *the earth. These are those who did not defile themselves*
> *with women, for they kept themselves pure. They follow*
> *the Lamb wherever he goes. They were purchased from*
> *among men and offered as firstfruits to God and the*
> *Lamb." (Revelation 14:1-4 NIV)*

Now, many Christian apologists will try their best to convince you that this number, 144,000 Jews, is not to be taken literally. But why should we accept it only as a symbolic number when the rest of John's writings suggest that he should be taken literally?

> *"I heard the number of those who were sealed, a hundred*
> *and forty-four thousand." (John 7:4)*

The number 144,000, we are told, equals 12,000 men multiplied by the twelve tribes of Israel. The phrase "those who were sealed" refers to a group of individuals who are selected from among mankind to rule with Jesus in Heaven. Moreover, the number, 144,000, is to be understood literally

198

for several reasons. Firstly, John further describes seeing in his vision a second group of people:

> *"A great crowd, which no man was able to number, out of all the nations and tribes and peoples and tongues."*
> *(John 7:4)*

It's important to note that the first group has a definite number, as opposed to the second, which is just said to be a "great crowd". This "great crowd' refers to those who will survive the coming "tribulation", which will destroy the then current sinful generation.

Most biblical scholars agree that this number is to be interpreted literally, and that John was adamant that the realms of Heaven would be reserved for Jewish male virgins only. Someone please pack the Ezy-Glide™!

All jokes aside, the New Testament is quite clear that only men shall enter the kingdom of heaven. Even some of the gospels, and epistles omitted by the Council of Nicaea have Jesus making this declaration outright, including the Gospel of Thomas, who writes that Jesus taught "every woman who makes herself male will enter the kingdom of heaven."

How the fuck does a woman accomplish this? With a strap on?

What do you think about that, ladies? I guess it doesn't make Paul's comment "It is disgraceful for a woman to speak in church" seem so bad by comparison.

The Big White Lie

Unfortunately, we've all had to attend at least one funeral in our lives. As for myself, I've been to several in the last few years, all were Christian burials. It was at the last funeral I attended, however, that it dawned on me that the Minister actively lied to all present when he said, "We can take comfort, as her faith in Jesus Christ as her savior means that she is now reunited with her husband, Bob, in heaven, who passed away 20 years prior." This, of course, was not the first time I'd heard these comforting words from those of the cloth, and no doubt you'll hear similar sentiments made at any of the thousands of Christian funerals taking place every day.

Notwithstanding the well-meaning intentions of the respective clergy that preside over funerals, my question is why do they lie to us? Is it their intention to deceive, or have they failed to read and or comprehend the 'ascension to heaven' related verses in the Bible?

Again, the Bible is very clear on the terms and conditions with respect to entry to afterlife; Jesus must return to earth riding atop a white fluffy cloud (really) in order to bring judgment upon mankind. Only at the conclusion of sorting the *"wheat from the chaff,"* will the righteous fly into heaven to reside by Jesus' side, with great marble mansions:

> *"In my Father's house are many rooms; if it were not so, I would have told you. I am going there to prepare a place for you. And if I go and prepare a place for you, I will come back and take you to be with me that you also may be where I am." (John 14:1-3)*

If you really believe that an eccentric head-case of a Jew, who has been dead for 2,000 years, will return to earth in such a manner, then you have a far greater imagination than I. I will leave you with the philosophical words of Christian Justin Martyr, who wrote in his book *'Second Apology'*:

> *"Those who have been persuaded that the unjust and intemperate shall be punished in eternal fire, but that the virtuous and those who lived like Christ shall dwell with God in a state that is free from suffering – we mean, those who have become Christians." (p520 Rome)*

In other words, according to the Christian doctrine, we non-believers, Buddhists, Muslims, Jews, Indigenous and Aboriginals, et al are destined for an ass reaming in Hell.

Christianity: "a religion of inclusive tolerance and solidarity"? I think not!

If the passage to Hell is paved with a rejection of the reported words of Jesus via his mystery biographers, then the following old joke stands as a beacon for rationality:

An Inuit hunter asked the local missionary priest: "If I did not know about God and sin, would I go to Hell?" "No," said the priest, "not if you did not know." "Then why," asked the Inuit earnestly, "did you tell me?"

Take a second to think about this joke, because in all seriousness, churches have sent missionaries to far off lands for hundreds of years, with intent to convert the barbarian heathens into Christians.

Some modern critics of the doctrine of Hell include Jonathan Kvanig, who wrote *The Problem of Hell*. He claims that even if Hell were seen as a choice rather than as punishment, it would be unreasonable for any kind of god, especially a supposedly all-loving one, to give such flawed primates as ourselves the incredible weight of responsibility of determining our own eternal destinies. Kvanig is a Christian, his belief is that a loving God would not abandon a person until they had made a rational, final decision, under favorable circumstances, to reject Jesus.

According to Kvanig, those who make decisions under duress, stress, or in a depression should be given a chance to make the 'right' decision at a time that all information is available for them to do so.

At the end of the day, people will routinely interpret the Bible to mean exactly what they want it to mean. There is equal support and denouncement of everything, you just need to find the right verse, quote it out of context, and bam, prostitution is legal and you're allowed ten slaves from neighboring nations… go for Mexicans though, they're better cooks.

Limbo

What of the billions of children who die a tragically premature death and never realize an opportunity to learn and or submit themselves to Jesus Christ? And what of the up to fifty percent of pregnancies which self-terminate? Well, the early Christian theologian St. Augustine concluded, in the fifth century, that infants who die without baptism were to be confined to the fires of Hell.

This became the belief of Christians for the next eight hundred years, although no passage in the Bible supported such supernatural speculation. By the 13th century, theologians referred to the "limbo of infants" as a place where un-baptized babies were deprived entrance into the gardens of heaven, and the sight of God, but did not suffer because they died not knowing of Jesus.

In 1983 the Code of Canon Law specified that, *"Children whose parents had intended to have them baptized but who died before baptism, may be allowed church funeral rites by the local ordinary."* How does the Church police the "intention"?

Then in our century, in 2007 in fact, the 30-member International Theological Commission revisited the ridiculous concept of limbo. The Catholic Commission of Cocks-in-frocks came away with no absolute determination of what happens to babies post-death. Imagine that, twenty first century university trained theologians are unable to determine what happens after death, according to the Christian faith, but yet over 2 billion people alive today will accept the ramblings of a likely illiterate schizophrenic tradesman from the first fucking century?

This doctrine portrays Christianity for what it truly is – a mish mash of ideas, ideals, ideologies and hopes, put in place by various committees. Committees who, in reality, had no idea of understanding any of what they purport to understand.

CHAPTER SIXTEEN

Why The Jews Didn't Believe Jesus Was The Messiah

This is a crucial question, especially when you consider we don't have independent, eyewitness accounts of Jesus, outside of the Bible and the non-canonized Gospels. Naturally, it's fair to assume that Jesus would have created some kind of publicity from his proclaimed miracles, and that these 'signs' would (or should) have been conclusive proof to all Jewish residents of the world at the time, that Jesus truly was the fulfillment of the Messianic prophecies.

But the Jewish priests, elders, and populace at large rejected Jesus wholly and fully. Obviously, this carries through to today whereby Judaism completely rejects the idea of Jesus being God, or a person of a Trinity, or even a mediator of God… most don't even believe that there was a historical Jesus.

From the Jewish perspective, Jesus had not fulfilled the prophecies of the Old Testament, and had fallen well short of embodying the qualifications of the Messiah foretold in Old Testament prophecy. It's fair to assume that the Jewish people should have known a Messiah when they saw one because THEY WROTE THE OLD TESTAMENT.

It amuses me whenever I have been in a room where an argument has erupted between a Christian and an Orthodox Jew, and the former says, "We know Jesus is the Son of God because he fulfilled the Messianic prophecies." To which the Jew replies, "Can you read Hebrew? Have you read the Tanakh? Well, don't tell us we are wrong when it was us that wrote the job description for the Messiah, and Jesus wasn't even in the same zip code!"

The term 'Messiah' is an English translation of the Hebrew "Mashiach", which means "Anointed One." According to the Old Testament it refers to a person initiated into God's service by being anointed with oil, and there are several vague passages which refer to this ceremony in Exodus 29:7, 1 Kings 1:39, II Kings 9:3. What the Hebrew Bible isn't vague on though is what it is that the Messiah is ordained to accomplish while here on earth, he is to:

1. Build the Third Temple

"I will make a covenant of peace with them; it will be an everlasting covenant. I will establish them and increase their numbers, and I will put my sanctuary among them forever. My dwelling place will be with them; I will be their God, and they will be my people. Then the nations will know that I the LORD make Israel holy, when my sanctuary is among them forever.'" (Ezekiel 37:26-28)

To save you the effort of counting, there were only two temples. The second destroyed by the Romans in 70 AD No new temple was ever rebuilt.

Jesus failed.

2. Gather all Jews back to the land of Israel

"Do not be afraid, for I am with you; I will bring your children from the east and gather from the west. I will say to the north, 'Give them up!' and to the south, 'Do not hold them back.' Bring my sons from afar and my daughters from the ends of the earth." (Isaiah 43:5-6)

Jesus failed.

3. Usher in an era of world peace, and end all hatred, oppression, suffering and disease.

"Nation shall not lift up sword against nation, neither shall man learn war anymore." (Isaiah 2:4)

Jesus really failed, dismally!

4. That the Hebrew God will be universally followed and therefore uniting humanity as one.

"God will be king over all the world – on that day, God will be the One and His Name will be One." (Zechariah 14:9)

Hahahahaha! Here's an experiment for you, go to your local happy-clapper Christian church this next weekend, stand in front of the congregation and announce to them that they are worshipping the same god as the Jews of Israel and the Muslims of Arabia. Here's a hint, wear a bulletproof vest! Jesus failed!

Failing to meet any of the four clear objectives above meant that the person failed to meet the expectation of the Messiah, as this was what God had promised to the prophets. Well, Jesus failed on all four of those objectives. No new temple, the Jews were scattered from their Holy Land, we are as far from world peace as we have ever been, and there are more than one billion Muslims who believe the world will one day bow to Mohammed and Allah.

To quote Stephen L Harris, Professor Emeritus of Humanities and Religious Studies at California State University and author of *The New Testament: A Student's Introduction:*

"Jesus did not accomplish what Israel's prophets said the Messiah was commissioned to do: He did not deliver the covenant people from their Gentile enemies, reassemble those scattered in the Diaspora, restore the Davidic kingdom, or establish universal peace. Instead of freeing Jews from oppressors and thereby fulfilling God's ancient

promises — for land, nationhood, kingship, and blessing — Jesus died a "shameful" death, defeated by the very political powers the Messiah was prophesied to overcome. Indeed, the Hebrew prophets did not foresee that Israel's savior would be executed as a common criminal by Gentiles, making Jesus' crucifixion a "stumbling block" to scripturally literate Jews.

Of course, Christian apologists have a rebuttal for everything. Nine times out of ten the counter argument is lunacy and fluff. The Jesus defense, a weak and hopeful one, is that Jesus WILL fulfill all of these objectives in his Second Coming. The same Second Coming promise that he is 1,900 years late on, and counting. Oh, and the same second coming that Paul predicted. Oh, and the same second coming that every bloody 'prophet', 'sage', and lunatic (notwithstanding Sarah Palin, George Bush and, well, most republicans) has also promised.

The conclusion that we are left with is so freaking simple, and we've alluded to it so many times throughout this book, that your forehead should be bruised face-palming yourself repeatedly; Jesus lied.

CHAPTER SEVENTEEN

Did Jesus Exist?

O k, we've uncovered the created mythology of Jesus Christ's life. The question is now; did such a man exist at all? Was there a Jesus of Nazareth, a man that lived, breathed, and wandered the Galilee countryside? This is a difficult question to answer, at least definitively. What we do know, based on much that we have covered, is that all sources about Jesus derive from hearsay accounts. Simply, no one has even a singular piece of physical evidence to support a historical Jesus; no artifacts, works, or self-written manuscripts. In other words, all claims about Jesus and his life are derived from the writings of other people. Devastating to Christian believers is that not a single contemporary writing makes mention of such a person, outside of documents proven to be fraudulent.

What appears most revealing of all comes not from what the New Testament authors wrote about him, but what historians and contemporaries did not write about him. Not a single historian, philosopher, or more significantly, one of his followers that lived during his time, makes any mention of him. None! It is this fact alone that is enough to convince Christopher Hitchens that the biblical Jesus is character of pure imagination.

Invariably Christian apologists will offer the factually flawed excuse that there were no prominent historians during that period, or the more fanciful apology that the Romans of Jerusalem were poor record keepers. These are both laughable assertions, as the Romans were astute record keepers, and Jerusalem was regarded as centre of education.

Now, Christians will throw forth the name Josephus Flavius as a non-Christian historian who wrote about Jesus, but this is as easy point to shoot down. Flavius is the earliest historian to mention Jesus, but scholars believe that his brief mentions of Jesus (in *Antiquities*) came from interpolations fraudulently penned by a later Church founder. Further, the date of Josephus' birth was 37 CE, at least several years after the alleged crucifixion of Jesus, thus making the premise he was an eyewitness a false one. Moreover, he wrote *Antiquities* in 93 CE, long after Mathew, Mark, and Luke had published their gospels. Therefore we can conclude that even if Josephus' brief mentions of Jesus were penned by him and not fraudulently added later, then we know that his information came to him second-hand, and therefore serves only as hearsay evidence.

At the end of the day, we have only after-the-event writings of Jesus, the writings we have examined in close detail, and not one of these writers gives a source or supports his claim with evidential material about the 'Savior'. As far as historians in that place at that time, there were many. One such example is the writings of Philo Judaeus, born in 20 BCE He is regarded as the preeminent Jewish-Hellenistic historian of Jesus' time and area. He wrote detailed accounts of Jewish events that took place within the Jerusalem and the surrounding regions. Not once does he ever mention the name Jesus. His silence is not isolated, as both Seneca (4 BCE – 65 CE) and Pliny the Elder (23 BCE – 79 CE) wasted not a single drop of ink in recording the life of Christianity's leading light.

Historian Jim Walker offered this anecdote in framing the absence of Jesus from any eyewitness historical documentation as such:

"Just imagine going through nineteenth century
literature looking for an Abraham Lincoln but unable to
find a single mention of him in any writing on earth until

the 20th century. Yet straight-faced Christian apologists and historians want you to buy a factual Jesus out of a dearth void of evidence, and rely on nothing but hearsay written well after his purported life. Considering that most Christians believe that Jesus lived as God on earth, the Almighty gives an embarrassing example for explaining his existence. You'd think a Creator might at least have the ability to bark up some good solid evidence."

Now, I have debated theists on the absence of evidence for Jesus' existence, and invariably the response comes back a little something like this, "If we use your historical standard then we can't prove also that Caesar, Alexander the Great, or Napoleon, existed." I hope you can see just how utterly absurd such a notion truly is. For all of these historical figures we have personal writings, artifacts, or eyewitness records, whereas, for the proclaimed Son of God we have *nada.* We have the equivalent of the hole in a donut.

Let's take a closer examination of Alexander the Great, for example, who preceded Jesus by nearly four centuries. For him we have signed treaties, and even a letter from him to the people of Chios, dated at 332 BCE What or Augustus Caesar? Well, for him we have the *Res gestae divi augusti,* a personal account of his own works and deeds. There is also a letter from him to his son, numerous eyewitness accounts and portraits. Sure, we have paintings of Jesus, but none were painted while he sat or stood before the artist. The fact the Bible makes no mention of Jesus' description is a further blow to the credibility of the claim that Jesus lived. One must think it odd that not a single record describes Jesus' appearance, outside of the account found in Josephus' records that were later proved fraudulent. In fact, it wasn't until a few hundred years after Jesus' death that the first images of what he looked like started to appear on the scene, which is why we have Jesus looking like anything from a Mid-West farmer's son to an Italian soccer player.

Ultimately, we are left with determining historical facts from hearsay. Facts derive out of evidence, and if one cannot support a hypothesis with evidence then it a hypothesis it remains. While this does not completely rule out any likelihood that the Jesus of the Bible lived, it is more likely probable that his biography was ramshackled together, borrowing mythologies from neighboring cultural centers. Stories that were incorporated into the Jesus Christ legend, including the virgin birth, walking on water, and resurrection were narratives familiar to numerous religious sects of that time and place.

While I personally am not sure one way or the other regarding the historicity of Jesus, many notable scholars continue to assert his life a complete fabrication. Some examples include:

John M Allegro, who argued in two books – *The Sacred Mushroom and the Cross* (1970) and *The Dead Sea Scrolls and the Christian Myth* (1979) – that Christianity began as a hallucinogenic mushroom consuming shamanic cult. In the latter books' foreword, Mark Hall writes:

> *"According to Allegro, the Jesus of the gospels is a fictional character in a religious legend, which like many similar tales in circulation at the turn of the era, was merely an amalgamation of Messianic eschatology and garbled historical events."*

GA Wells, Emeritus Professor at Birkbeck College, London, and author of *Did Jesus Exist?* (1975), *The Jesus Legend* (1996), *The Jesus Myth* (1999), *Can We Trust the New Testament* (2004), and *Cutting Jesus Down to Size* (2009). Wells writes that there are three broad approaches to the historicity of Jesus:

> 1. *That Jesus is almost or entirely fictional.*
> 2. *That he did exist but that reports about him are so saturated by myth that very little can be said of him with any confidence.*

3. *That he not only existed, but that a core of
    historical facts can be disclosed about him*

Wells believes that the truth lay somewhere between
points 1 and 2.

Timothy Freke & Peter Gandy, British co-authors of
The Jesus Mysteries (1999) and *The Laughing Jesus* (2005)
argue that the Gospels *"can tell us nothing at all about an
historical Jesus because no such man existed."* They claim that
early Christians created Jesus as a Jewish version of an
amalgam of dying and rising gods.

Jesus, if there ever really was a historical Jesus and I do
doubt that there was, was nothing more than a
schizophrenic, uppity asshole whose claim to fame was
nothing more than pissing off the ruling Jewish authority,
then getting killed because of it. Were it not for a series of
good publicists, some very talented PR work and the work
of the Emperor Constantine, the memory of Jesus would
have decomposed, along with his flesh, TWO
THOUSAND FUCKING YEARS AGO!

But don't let that deter your faith!

DID JESUS EXIST?

Afterword

Evidence of Jesus' biographical architecture, throughout the New Testament, is right there for all to see… if you're willing to open your eyes. Separating fact from fiction and biography from bullshit isn't nearly as difficult as you may have guessed prior to reading this rudimentary level examination of the Holy authors. Hopefully, like me, you will have the appetite to dig deeper – each shovel of information striking painful blows to a socially retarding man made ancient belief, that is Christianity, or any other religion for that matter.

Teaching our children to look for and ask for the evidence, to question everything, and to think critically are among the most valuable lessons that we can teach. Doing so can only improve the conditions that underlie our incredible civilization.

History has proven time and time again that bad things happen when large chunks of the demographic believe what they're told *absolutely* and with unwavering blind faith. Do we really want to return to a time where religion rules, and rationality, logic and actual morality take a back seat to "Thou shall worship no gods before me"? It's those conditions that harvest political despots. Surely, eight years of Bush has taught us to not be so blindsided again.

Despite what we've discovered in this book, we can always be sure that the Christian-Right is waiting diligently patiently for their next Messiah. Then again, if Jesus' own disciples didn't get to see him again after Jesus had said, in no uncertain terms, that he'd return, Republican or not, you're ultimately left with two chance, none and none.

Christianity, like its gassy uncle Judaism, and its naughty nephew with ADD, Islam, contains no mystery. It's not a journey into the unknown, and people shouldn't treat it as such. The facts for its creation are evident. We have the facts. This book did not find the gunman who shot Kennedy; it only presented what scholars present as verified fact, and the passages of the Bible itself. There was no magic to this, no miracles, no visions or speaking in tongues. I wish I could tell you there was, but there really, truly, plainly wasn't.

Sociologists have demonstrated in numerous studies that societies move towards religious belief when placed under collective stress. The post 9-11 America was a great example of this. Similarly, in the decades prior to the first century, the Jews prophesized and hungered for a Messiah, a deliverer that would restore their former glory, a time when Jerusalem and the Holy Land was theirs.

The phrase "the end times" was a common meme told as a means to inspire and provide comfort to the Jewish people, while they lived in a nation occupied by their Roman overlords. Many Jews believed a final war at God's behest would see the destruction and end to the Roman occupation. No doubt it is this sentiment that ignited the flame for the future growth of Christianity.

We know that the early Christians lived within pagan communities, and therefore it is of little surprise or coincidence that many of the Hellenistic and pagan myths parallel so closely to the mythology of Jesus.

One such example is the religion of Zoroaster, founded more than five centuries before Jesus' alleged arrival, a religion that began in Persia. The cornerstones of this faith were rooted in the belief of a celestial heaven and afterlife, a last judgment, and resurrection of the dead.

Similarly, Osiris, Hercules, Mithra, Hermes, Prometheus, Perseus and others compare to the Christian's mythical fairytale. They are epic tales, which describe very similar feats of incredulity, but 85% of Americans don't believe in them. Patrick Campbell, in *The Mythical Jesus*, highlights the similarities of the more topical myths of Hercules, Mirtha, Hermes, and Osiris:

"All served as pre-Christian sun gods, yet all allegedly had gods for fathers, virgins for mothers; had their births announced by stars; got born on the solstice around December 25th; had tyrants who tried to kill them in their infancy; met violent deaths; rose from the dead; and nearly all got worshiped by "wise men" and had allegedly fasted for forty days. [McKinsey, Chapter 5]

Saint Justin Martyr, second century apologist, was at least intellectually honest enough to recognize the analogies between Christianity and Paganism. To the Pagans, he wrote:

"When we say that the Word, who is first born of God, was produced without sexual union, and that he, Jesus Christ, our teacher, was crucified and died, and rose again, and ascended into heaven; we propound nothing different from what you believe regarding those whom you esteem sons of Jupiter (Zeus)." [First Apology, ch. Xxi]

I think that adequately illustrates the evidence for this religion's creation. For the benefit of brevity I will leave you with the Bertrand Russell's profoundly brilliant summary to a speech he gave in London in 1928:

"We want to stand upon our own feet and look fair and square at the world – its good facts, its bad facts, its beauties, and its ugliness; see the world as it is and be not afraid of it. Conquer the world by intelligence and not merely by being slavishly subdued by the terror that comes from it. The whole conception of a God is a conception derived from the ancient oriental despotisms. It is a conception quite unworthy of free men. When you hear people in church debasing themselves and saying that they are miserable sinners, and all the rest of it, it seems contemptible and not worthy of self-respecting human beings. We ought to stand up and look the world frankly in the face. We ought to make the best we can of the world, and if it is not as good as we wish, after all it will still be better than what these others have made of it in all these ages. A good world needs knowledge, kindliness, and courage; it does not need a regretful hankering after the past or a fettering of the free intelligence by the words uttered long ago by ignorant men. It needs a fearless outlook and a free intelligence. It needs hope for the future, not looking back all the time toward a past that is dead, which we trust will be far surpassed by the future that our intelligence can create."

Hope you enjoyed the read, and are now able to see Christianity for what it is – a melting pot of ideology handcrafted by a great number of men, none of whom ever met or knew the living Jesus. The question is – will the evidence thus presented sway Christians from their belief? Perhaps; or perhaps not!

That said, if you remain a believer then I suggest you continue to sin because I hate to see a life go to waste. And if you don't sin, Jesus died for nothing.

Bibliography

INTRODUCTION

End of Faith, Sam Harris

CHAPTER ONE

Mere Christianity, CS Lewis

Speech, Bertrand Russell

CHAPTER TWO

Rome & Jerusalem, Martin Goodman

Jesus Interrupted, Bart D Ehrman

Modelling Early Christianity, Esler, Routledge p.129

History of God, Karen Armstrong

Losing Faith in Faith, Dan Barker

CHAPTER THREE

God is Not Great, Christopher Hitchens

The Treaties of God, HL Mencken

Age of Reason, Thomas Paine

CHAPTER FOUR

The Historical Basis of the Jesus Legend, Hayyim ben Yehoshu

Jesus, AN Wilson

Herod the Great, Michael Grant

Is Christianity True?, M Arnhiem, Prometheus Books, 1984

G Ernest Wright of Harvard Divinity School (1960)

The Unauthorized Version: Truth and Fiction in the Bible,
Robin Lane Fox

CHAPTER SIX

Christians and the Holy Places, J Taylor, Clarendon Press, 1993, p.265

God is Not Great, Christopher Hitchens

Essay: Saint Mark Says They Mustn't, Barry Qualls

CHAPTER SEVEN

The Historical Evidence of Jesus, GA Wells

Farewell to God: My reasons for rejecting the Christian faith, Charles Templeton

Miracles and Idolatry, Voltaire

God is Not Great, Christopher Hitchens

CHAPTER EIGHT

Jesus Interrupted, Bart D Ehrman

CHAPTER NINE

The Historical Evidence of Jesus, GA Wells

The Holocaust as Interruption, Florenza & Tracy Edinburg, T&T Clark Ltd, 1984

Anti-Semitism and the Foundations of Christianity, Rev. James Parkes Paulist Press, New York, 1979 p.xi

CHAPTER TWELVE

Misquoting Jesus, Bart D Ehrman

Adam, Eve, and the Serpent, Elaine Pagels, Professor of Religion at Princeton University

Me of Little Faith, Lewis Black

The Greatest Show on Earth, Richard Dawkins, Bantam Press, p.6

The Antichrist, Nietzsche

CHAPTER FOURTEEN

Robert G Ingersoll

The Problem of Hell, Robert Kvanig

CHAPTER FIFTEEN

The New Testament: A Student's Introduction, Stephen L Harris

BY THE SAME AUTHOR
www.dangerouslittlebooks.com

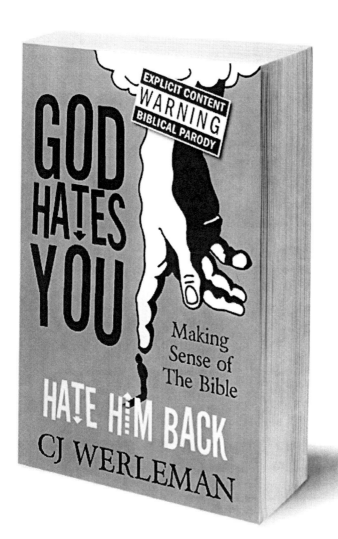

FOLLOW THE AUTHOR
www.cjwerleman.com

LaVergne, TN USA
15 October 2010
200991LV00004B/51/P